EXTRAORDINARY ORDINARY WOMEN
~ OF SOUTH WILTSHIRE

For Nick and Verity, with all my love

and for Lucas, Brodie, Sam, Maeve, Iver, Joshua, Frankie, Theo, Joel, and Albert – the next generation, whom I hope to inspire.

Illustrated by Lucia Lovatt **https://www.paintingsbylucia.co.uk/**

Extraordinary Ordinary *Women*

~ *of South Wiltshire*

LUCY WHITFIELD

THE HOBNOB PRESS

First published in the United Kingdom in 2025

by The Hobnob Press,
8 Lock Warehouse, Severn Road, Gloucester GL1 2GA
www.hobnobpress.co.uk

© Lucy Whitfield 2025

The Author hereby asserts her moral rights to be identified as the Author of the Work.

All rights reserved. No part of this publication may be reproduced, stored in a retrieval system, or transmitted in any form or by any means, electronic, mechanical, photocopying, recording or otherwise, without the prior permission of the publisher and copyright holder.

British Library Cataloguing in Publication Data
A catalogue record for this book is available from the British Library

ISBN 978-1-918403-01-5

Typeset in Chaparral Pro, 11/14 pt
Typesetting and origination by John Chandler

Contents

Acknowledgements

Introduction	1
Susannah Tadd	5
Lizzie Hilda Hay	9
Christian Hamilton	21
Helen and Grace Bagnall	28
West Lavington Ladies' Football Team	39
Elise Possart or Hassan	47
Emma Bown and Ann Freemantle, both later called Goodfellow	56
Dorcas Clark or Pearce/Pierce	66
Amy Aylward	75
Freelove Priscilla Noad or Wastfield or Sims	82
Susannah Smith	90
Dorothy May Lodge	96
Jane Goodfellow or Shore	103
Thirza Newman, Harriet Judd or Sutton, and friends	109
Ellen Pengelly or Yipsing	118
Bessy Gramlick or McClintock	126
Martha Bennett	132
Index	140
About the author	145

Acknowledgements

THANKS FOR SUPPORT, energy and enthusiasm go to Louise and John of Hobnob, for their encouragement and help in putting this book together, and to Lucia for wonderful artwork, coaching, caffeine and mentoring. To Julie, Ruth, Heather and all the other wonderful staff at Wiltshire and Swindon History Centre who've aided many of my discoveries; to Elaine, Melissa and all the team (past and present) at Chippenham Museum; and Sue, Penny, Lisa, Hannah and the rest of the team at Chippenham Library for providing support and a nurturing space. To Chris Dallimore for his knowledge, kindness and willingness to be a sounding board. To Heather for stout-soaked heritage chats, and the Arkinstalls-next-door for being so encouraging. To far too many friends - Helen, Dan & Jenny, Laura, Bettina, Chris, Fi, Andy, Malc, Lou, and the banquet crew (and I've probably forgotten someone again), and all music/dance/journalist friends far and wide. To Cina and Mike at Cousin Normans for incredible coffee and a warm and welcoming work space; Linds at the Old Road Tavern for giving me great cider and an extension to my living room; and Bryan at Wine Monkey for a lovely venue and giving History Portal Club a home. To the people of Wiltshire for absorbing me, entrancing me, and letting me tell the stories of your county, and to everyone who's taken the time to tell me about their granny. Or maiden aunt. And who has believed that their female relative could be more than just a name on a family tree. Lastly, thanks and love go to immediate family, all parents, siblings, and cousins, whether by blood or in-law. And finally, to my partner Nick and daughter Verity for their love and unwavering support for the career I'm making for myself.

Lucy Whitfield

Introduction

PEOPLE DON'T FIT into neat little boxes.
None of the women included in this book ever gave any thought to whether they'd conveniently fit into a collection of Wiltshire women over a century later if they'd just stayed an Amesbury resident a bit longer. Why would they?

They just got on with their lives, and did what they needed to do, in the place that felt right to them, regardless of any geography or attempt to achieve anything out of the ordinary.

It's us, or rather the author and editor, who have to decide whether they fit into a particular remit of doing enough in South Wiltshire to fit the geographical boundaries of this collection, and then further evaluate what they got up to in their lives to fit the idea of what an extraordinary ordinary woman might be.

And, as with the first collection of stories of women from North Wiltshire, having a story that involves suffrage or STEM achievement is not necessarily an identifying criterion for an extraordinary ordinary woman either, as might be assumed from the way women's history has traditionally been taught or latterly written about.

Each of the women included in the book has been investigated against these thoughts to produce a broad swathe of women's experiences in the past. All, at least at the time of writing and researching, have flown under the radar thus far and not been widely disseminated. The one slight exception is Helen Bagnall, who was discovered and blogged about in early 2018 by my Women Who Made Me project, but was picked up by Salisbury researchers later that year and has gained a slightly wider profile.

Some fantastic women's stories were unearthed in the course of researching and writing this book, but were ultimately not pursued because they didn't quite hit the right note with any part of the remit.

For example, an author would have been a great woman to include, and to that end several were identified.

Frothy Edwardian romance serial author Sybil Campbell Lethbridge lived in Melksham for a while during the Second World War. She had an interesting and unconventional family background and personal life, and was involved in women's suffrage too. But ultimately she carried out the most interesting bits of her life in Kensington, so was laid aside as she didn't fit the geography well enough.

The author and compiler of the Women's Suffrage Cookbook, 'Mrs Aubrey Dowson' aka Phillis, also retired to a village just north of Salisbury in her later years. But again, her story really took place in the Midlands and in transit around the world, so she was laid aside too.

Another author, Maud Frances Davies, was a sociologist and campaigner, and wrote a social study on the village of Corsley, where her father was based – that some felt lacked the right degree of empathy. But, where there is a reasonable body of evidence available about her life, her 1913 death in a London Tube tunnel is far more interesting and has been discussed at length by true crime authors. Since this collection focuses on lives rather than demises, she was put aside too.

And Girls' Own fiction author Phyllis I Norris, from Salisbury, was another candidate for inclusion, and hit the spot geographically as she'd never lived anywhere else. But, though she'd published 11 books about plucky young women in the 1940s and 1950s, she didn't appear to write anything of note – or do anything to bring herself to the fore – for the following 40 years. Unless she wrote under a pseudonym, which hasn't come to light either. Again, she didn't make the cut.

Each of these weren't quite right, for their own reasons, and ultimately an author hasn't made the pages of this book. But, as ever with women's history, it's important not to look at what you haven't got, and instead uncover and seek to value what you do have.

Valuing women's history begins at the grassroots level, by actively encouraging everyone to get knee-deep in their own female ancestry as well as those women traditionally lauded. To that end, each of these women's stories are told in the most accessible language possible, to open the door so everyone can step inside. After all, women's stories don't just live in ivory towers or archives; they're woven into kitchen tables, factory floors, and neighbourhood gossip. This breathes warmth and down-to-earth storytelling into the extraordinary ordinary women's lives uncovered, and hopefully acts as an incentive and encouragement to find more, rooting those stories where they belong — among the people who lived them and those who still carry them. History should breathe in local voices and be told in a way where everyone gets to see themselves in the narrative.

Those who have been included in this book cover women from south of Salisbury, through to communities on the rivers that run into that town and women who walked its streets and taught in its schools. There are a couple from Warminster, working north towards Trowbridge and Bradford-on-Avon, and then stretching east across the county to Seend and West Lavington and beyond.

There is a woman who divorced her husband at the first moment she was able to, a Prussian steam laundry manageress, a Japanese butler's partner, a cloth weaver who married up, a girls' school teacher who taught abroad, a suffrage organisation secretary, a soprano singer, a dog breeder, and a clutch of footballers banned from playing, among others. As with the previous volume on North Wiltshire, the idea has been to cover many facets of women's past experiences over the last two or three centuries.

And, if we uncover and write about women's history, are we celebrating these women?

Books aimed at popularising women's history, like Kate Pankhurst's *Fantastically Great Women Who Changed The World* or Elena Favilli & Francesca Cavallo's *Good Night Stories For Rebel Girls*, seem to give that impression in a general sense – that we are profiling women's achievements in a society that left them behind, and they should therefore be celebrated for these.

Instead, this collection sidesteps slightly, to look at the true nitty gritty of ordinary women's lives. Occurrences that are not necessarily achievements but the realities and experiences that were nonetheless very present in the past. To that end, the collection also looks at sex workers, women who concealed unwanted pregnancies, those less interested in motherhood than a 'true woman' was felt should be at that time, criminals, women suffering mental health issues.

There may be those who – backing the idea that celebrating achievement, and profiling suffrage and STEM activities are the right approach with women's history to put the genre on a more equal footing with the way history has traditionally been taught and presented – feel these subjects are uneasy bedfellows and perhaps better suited for collections with a different remit.

However, to be truly human is to know that people are flawed, that women aren't inherently nice across the board, that difficult subjects are just as much a part of a full life experience as those held up as worthy achievements. This approach, though not populist, takes in the fuller picture.

Again, women's history does not fall into neat little boxes. It is sprawling, messy, unpredictable, occurring in multiple arenas, and at its very root not quite what you'd expect it to be.

Susannah Tadd

ONE OF THE ways women who had an illegitimate child could attempt to get support in Victorian times was to pursue the father of the child through the courts, and ask for him to pay regularly for the child's upkeep.

However, if the woman involved was felt not to have been repentant or was perceived as completely fallen, that same court could decide that she deserved no support from the father whatsoever. This was the case with Susannah Tadd, who pursued Simon Hobbs – the father of her child – and petitioned via the petty sessions for financial support in 1864. Despite evidence from Susanna's brother's lover, the court refused this request because Susannah had been the mother of six illegitimate children, and therefore was of poor moral fibre. They dismissed the case because of this.

Six illegitimate children would appear to be going it some, for the period, and the verdict completely judgemental, but Susannah appears to have lived a rather unconventional life with regard to sexual and marital morals at that time – which would have been the reason for the moralising tone and disparaging nature of newspaper reports that featured her.

Simon Hobbs – who at the time was caught up in the courts for other reasons too (poaching, trespass, and general roughhousing, in one case also involving Susannah's brother) – was apparently heard to say by Miss Spender, Susannah's brother's lover, that if he wasn't standing on these charges he would not mind paying for the child. This child was his and Susannah's son George, but he does not appear to have been the father of her other five children. Most of these were little boys, several also named George, who did not live very long.

Susannah was born in Westwood, a small community just outside Bradford-on-Avon in Wiltshire in about 1835. She was one of at least nine children, and her parents – John and Ann - were agricultural labourers. In early adulthood she left home and found work as a servant, sometimes in Bath, and sometimes in the small communities surrounding that city.

Her first son, William George Tadd, was born in July 1853, when she was around 18, and three subsequent boys named George followed in 1857, 1858 and 1859. The Georges died at 18 months, eight months and four months respectively. A daughter – Elizabeth –was born in the summer of 1861 but lived for four months, and then the fifth boy – also George – in the winter of 1863/4. This would appear to be the child that she attempted to take the father to court over. Only William and the last George seem to have survived childhood.

She does not appear to have been the only member of her family who indulged in relationships that were against the public perception of decency for the time. Her brother also had a partner he wasn't married to, who had two illegitimate children.

Having failed to convince the courts of her entitlement to support for her son, and her relationship with Simon having waned, Susannah took up with someone else. This time her paramour was a married man, Samuel Love, whose official relationship had run its course. However, divorce in the 1860s was very difficult to obtain so dissatisfied couples would often live apart. He'd been married to Sarah Powell since 1850, and they had a son together, but Samuel had taken up with Susannah, and by 1867 they were cohabiting.

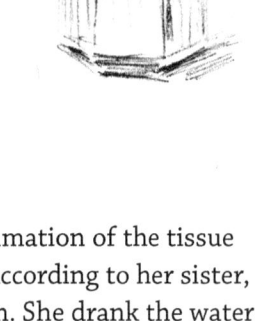

The inevitable happened, and Susannah ended up pregnant again. Or, as the disparaging and moralising tone of the *Wiltshire Times and Trowbridge Advertiser* euphemistically put it, 'she found herself in a fair way to increase the pauper population.'

Some months into the pregnancy, Susannah was suffering from pleurisy – an inflammation of the tissue between the lungs and the ribcage. Her partner, according to her sister, mixed her some pepper and water to ease the pain. She drank the water but left the pepper, according to reports.

Around six months into the pregnancy, after an evening that involved her brother William, her lover Samuel, her brother's lover (who wasn't named in newspaper reports) and a bottle of gin, Susannah went into premature labour at seven months gestation. The result was premature twins, a boy and a girl, who were too under-developed to survive, but were nevertheless born alive.

Susannah asked her neighbour, Ann Gerrish, to bury the newborn boy and girl in the garden, but her neighbour struggled with this instruction – despite the reward that Susannah promised her – given the children were still alive. Susannah's sister Amelia, who was around at the time, urged her to complete the job, but Ann immediately went back to Susannah, and refused to bury the babies. She began to wash them, but both died during this process as they were too premature.

Shortly after this, Susannah died, after the physical strains involved in giving birth to the twins. Local rumour suspected that Samuel Love had poisoned her in order to abort the babies, and a court case followed.

It was discovered that Susannah had no trace of any abortifacient in her system, and the cause of death was double pleurisy. And that the twins were too immature to have survived, at least with the medical care available at the time. A death from natural causes was recorded.

About five years later, in the Autumn of 1872, Samuel also died, by drowning in the Kennet and Avon canal at Devizes. He had become a boatman on the canal, but he slipped while crossing a lock across the water, near Prisoner and Foxhanger bridges, probably one on the Caen Hill flight, and struck his head against the stonework as he fell. He and his wife Sarah appear to have separated completely as a result of his relationship with Susannah, and their son Thomas was being brought up elsewhere.

Susannah's son George became a groom, then went into the army in 1885. Her son William lived in Cardiff and worked in the coal trade.

References

England & Wales, Civil Registration Birth Index, 1837-1915, held by Ancestry.co.uk

England & Wales, Civil Registration Marriage Index, 1837-1915, held by Ancestry.co.uk

England & Wales, Civil Registration Death Index, 1837-1915, held by Ancestry.co.uk

Trowbridge Chronicle, 30 April 1864, Petty Session: Affiliation Case

Trowbridge Chronicle, 28 November 1863, Petty Sessions: Trespass in pursuit of

game
UK Census collection, held by Ancestry.co.uk
UK, Royal Hospital Chelsea Pensioner Soldier Service Records, 1760-1920, held by Ancestry.co.uk
Warminster Herald, 12 October 1872, Devizes
Wiltshire, England, Church of England Births and Baptisms, 1813-1922, held by Ancestry.co.uk
Wiltshire, England, Church of England Marriages and Banns, 1754-1916, held by Ancestry.co.uk
Wiltshire, England, Church of England Deaths and Burials, 1813-1922 held by Ancestry.co.uk
Wiltshire, England, Marriages, 1538-1837, held by Ancestry.co.uk
Wiltshire Independent, 25 April 1867, Bradford on Avon: Suspected Poisoning Case
Wiltshire Times and Trowbridge Advertiser, 30 April 1864, Bradford on Avon: Petty Sessions
Wiltshire Times and Trowbridge Advertiser, 20 April 1867, Bradford on Avon: Extraordinary deaths at Westwood

Lizzie Hilda Hay

VOCATIONAL EDUCATION COMES in and out of style in British society. Initially any sort of formal education whatsoever was the preserve of rich young boys – for example, Tudor-founded grammar schools – but it could be argued that during this period girls and children from lower classes were receiving a type of vocational education, as they were being trained on the job for the role they were expected to have in life.

Today's children are mostly expected to receive an academic education to a point – GCSE level – but after that are allowed to specialise in vocational education if they wish (although there's considerable pressure to continue the academic route if at all possible, with more societal value placed upon it). In the late 1940s and onwards that split was earlier, and vocational subjects came into play after the age of 11 with grammar schools, secondary moderns, and the much-less remembered technical schools separating the focus. In later Victorian times, after education became compulsory until the age of 11 (1893) or later 12 (1899), the vocational subjects came in even earlier – boys were taught joinery and building skills, girls were trained in the domestic arts. The how and what and why of education in each era has always been based on the life that the surrounding society believes that those children are due to lead, and that's as applicable today as it was in the 19th century.

And, in the early 20th century, when Lizzie Hilda Hay became principal of the Wiltshire School of Cookery and Domestic Economy, the life of most ordinary young women was supposed to include a high chance of domestic service. With marriage still seen as the highest goal for women, there was also a definite probability of housewifery and running a household, so encouraging good domestic skills was an important part of girls' education. Many girls would undertake domestic skills training during their final year at school, which were centrally organised in different Wiltshire towns by the school based in Trowbridge.

Lizzie, or Hilda (as she preferred to be known) was the sixth and final principal of the school, appointed in 1919. She was the longest serving, totting up 26 years in the role before the school finally shut, and presided over the period of greatest social change.

Hilda came from the Chorlton area, near Manchester, but had deep Scottish ancestry. Her father, James Shaw Hay, was a cotton merchant at the time of her June 1881 birth, and her mother, Charlotte Augusta Corlett, was the daughter of a successful builder. Both had been born on the Isle of Man. Her parents, though James had an aristocratic background, were part of a booming upper middle class who were living on the profits of successful manufacturing industries. Her father James should not be confused with Sir James Shaw Hay (1839-1924), who was former governor of Sierra Leone, Liberia, The Gambia and Barbados, and was a non-close relative. Hilda's father James was directly dealing with buying cotton from the East India Company, which – despite not being in charge of India by 1881 – was still very much involved in the trade of Indian cotton.

Hilda was their first child, followed by two younger brothers, Conran – who eventually emigrated to Canada – and Thomas. Though all being born around Manchester, and having a residence in Didsbury, the family seemed to spend a large amount of time on the Isle of Man while Hilda was growing up. It was where her father James was born, and the air quality was probably better for bringing up children rather than that found in the industrial areas around Manchester. James would have been able to catch a boat back from the island to Liverpool to reach his business interests in Manchester.

Their mother, Charlotte, died at Ramsey on the Isle of Man in 1886 aged 35, when Hilda was only five years old, and her brothers were toddlers. Their father remarried, to Arminal Walmesley Scotson, in 1889, and they were joined by younger half-sister Muriel in 1892. The family were resident on Lord Street in Withington by 1891.

By 1901, though, Hilda was 19 and unoccupied, having finished any education she had received. This was nothing out of the ordinary for young women of her class at this time – they spent their time at home, attending social functions and time was given to finding them the right partner to eventually marry. Her father was still buying cotton from India, as the cotton industry in Manchester was yet to decline, and her two younger brothers were employed as junior clerks in a bank and a merchant business.

Something changed for her in the following years, however. Either that expected marriage had not come along or she didn't actually want it in the first place, or she was dissatisfied with her lot in life – as unmarried and educated women of her class background were beginning to explore other avenues. She began to train as a dressmaking and millinery teacher in 1905. The other catalyst for this may have been her father's health being in decline (he died in 1908) as the family's lifestyle may have needed extra funds to continue.

Hilda went to the Municipal School of Technology in Manchester for a year to study to become a teacher in dressmaking. She also added an evening school teachers' domestic economy certificate in dressmaking, millinery (the making of hats) and needlework. That Manchester school had developed out of the Manchester Mechanics' Institute in 1883, and had offered a range of technical courses to meet the needs of the industrial area. At the time Hilda attended, courses could lead to degrees at the Victoria University of Manchester, but she seems not to have gone down that route, instead heading into teaching herself. She would have studied at the Sackville Building, which became part of University of Manchester Institute of Science and Technology (UMIST).

Once trained, Hilda went to work in various technical roles around the area. She taught dressmaking at the Women's and Girl's Institute in Manchester, which specialised in giving girls from a mill background new skills, and also to young women at the Hyde Technical School. She also taught millinery and needlework at Gorton Domestic School at the same time. Later on, she taught more millinery at various elementary schools across Mossley and Heaton Norris in Lancashire.

The 1911 census finds her living in the Moss Side area of inner Manchester with her widowed stepmother, employed as a teacher by the Manchester Education committee. Her younger half-sister was also in the household, working as a governess for a private family so bringing in a wage. There were also two paying guests in the household, both of them Swiss businessmen. This points to a household that needed extra money to function, so whatever reason Hilda had in the first place for becoming a teacher, her wages were very much needed. At the time, her recently married brother Conran was a secretary for a cotton mill, and her other brother Thomas was a merchant and living elsewhere.

In 1913, round about the time she moved into her thirties, Hilda left the family and the Manchester area, and took a job teaching dressmaking, millinery and needlework at the Training School of Domestic Science in Bath. The classes there were in a north extension of the main Guildhall, now the seat of Bath and North East Somerset council, and the school offered things like household and high class cookery, laundry work, dress making, stitchery and ornamental needlework. Hilda would have joined a highly skilled team of teachers.

After a year though, she'd made another move, this time to Trowbridge, where she became teacher of dressmaking and needlework at the Wiltshire Domestic School. And it is then that her long association with the school began.

Like many of the other places where Hilda had taught, the Wiltshire Domestic School was set up in the later 19th century to help improve the basic skills of the working population. This included industrial workers, who attended classes in the evenings, and children in the top years of elementary schools. The school leaving age was 11 until 1899 and 12 thereafter, and in Standard VI, the top year of that provision (providing the child had not passed an exam to go to grammar school), the girls received instruction and classes that were linked to the domestic school – dress making, laundry work, various cookery, household economy, and so on, in addition to things like knitting and needlework that had been taught throughout their schooling.

The Wiltshire school was begun in 1891. It had been agitated for by various prominent women in the county for a few years, pointing out that boys would receive some technical education as part of their apprenticeship at workplaces, but there was no similar provision available for girls. Grants were made, and the school set up, opening in April 1892. Girls aged 14 and upwards, having left elementary school, could receive three months training in cookery and household duties for a small fee. The school also ran courses to train elementary school teachers in various subjects in the holidays, so these could be taken back to their communities and taught to their pupils. And there was also provision for training new teachers on site too.

The first head, or superintendent, of the school was Alice Bridgman, an innkeepers' daughter from Devon who had previously been a private governess. Initially the school was in three buildings in 'an out of the way part of the town' according to the *Marlborough Times* in 1896, but the exact premises haven't come to light. By 1896 it had moved to a new home at 4 Fore Street in Trowbridge, and received a grand opening from Lady Lucy Hicks-Beach, who lived out at Netheravon. This space allowed everything (housewifery, millinery, laundry, cookery, dressmaking, sewing) under one roof, and enabled the school to take in boarders with ease. By 1901 there were nine boarders, girls from all over Wiltshire, ranging in age from 14 to 18.

Alice Bridgman left in 1904, to found her own domestic service school back in Devon, and Mary Edith Casement took over the head of the school role. Daughter of a plumber, and from Liverpool originally, she'd been on the staff since at least 1899 and had previously taught music before taking on domestic subjects. She had originally intended to leave herself to head to Aberdeenshire, until offered the headship. Under her leadership, the range of subjects available expanded to include sweet making and home upholstery. She was also authorised by the council to begin to inspect the standards of domestic subject teaching in communities all over Wiltshire as part of the role, so the job took on a travelling element. And conferences of domestic teachers were beginning to be held too, with the school upheld as the high standard to aspire towards. Magistrate's wife Emily Fuller, who lived at Neston Park and was part of the Hicks-Beach family, was extremely prominent in this process and supported the school throughout its existence.

Miss Casement eventually left in 1907, initially to a similar school in Folkestone in Kent and then to Aberdeenshire with her special friend Louisa. The school then had a Miss Adcock at the helm for a year, followed by Mary Smith who also held the role only briefly. Mary Smith had come up from a similar position in a school in Dorset. Under her, the grant for the school from the county council was due to end, and with it the lease to the premises in Fore Street. There was a proposed move, backed by Emily Fuller, to re-site the school in Salisbury, but funds and new premises were found in Trowbridge. The school moved to Laurel Bank on Hilperton Road which had previously been in the possession of William Applegate. These would have been the buildings that Hilda came to when she joined the school a few years later. The school opened there in December 1909, and aimed to be self-supporting, with no more training of county teachers. Instead, ladies could apply for courses to further their skills, and the school offered scholarships to girls leaving elementary schools. The inspection role still remained.

The new constitution of the school was reflective of the national drive towards continuing education into teenage years, with it summed up in the *Wiltshire Times* in July 1910:

> The object is to provide a thorough training in domestic duties and the general management of a household, suited for women and girls of all classes, and not merely to afford a training to girls who are intending to enter domestic service. Such a course of instruction should form an indispensable part of every girl's education. It should be clearly understood that the instruction given is in no way limited to manual work, but includes a large among of teaching of a generally educational character intended to train the mind and develop the intelligence of the pupils.

Mary Smith left at some point during 1910, and was replaced by Katherine Agnes Willson, who was the principal who employed Hilda in the school in the first place. The 1911 census has her at Laurel Bank, with two teachers, a matron, three ladies receiving instruction and 23 boarding students aged between 14 and 16. Katherine, though born in Sussex, had grown up in Bradford-on-Avon as the daughter of a chemist, and had taken up domestic subject teaching as the 20th century began, training at the Wiltshire School of Cookery and Domestic Economy herself from 1902. She'd taught laundry work, housewifery and cookery at the school throughout her time there, and had been a visiting teacher at various elementary schools. Hilda took up her employment with Katherine at some point during 1914.

There was a wavering of local opinion during the First World War as to whether a school of cookery and domestic economy was still needed, with women being encouraged into more traditional male roles in the workforce, and a drop off in the hiring of domestic servants, as many felt this was a complete change that would continue. Katherine, Hilda and the school were part of an argument put forth by Emily Fuller at conferences that there was no greater need at any time in history for training in domestic economy, as many of the soldiers were predicted to come back injured and therefore with less earning capacity, so household budgets would get tighter. However, dwindling numbers meant that the school struggled to survive, and even with Mrs Fuller's optimism, it was marked for closure in July 1917.

What saved the school was the establishment of food management as the war went into 1917 and food stocks dwindled. The staff and students of the Wiltshire Cookery School, as it was affectionately shortened to, were involved in the food economy depot set up in Fore Street, and their expertise in food and budget management was drawn upon. The closure was halted, and new scholarships announced for September 1917.

Katherine Willson decided to leave the school after the end of the war, and departed in 1919 for a similar position in Chelmsford, Essex, and Hilda took up the headship. She was to become the school's longest standing principal.

The upping of the minimum school leaving age from 12 to 14 in 1918 did not really affect the school, as the scholarships required the attending girls to be under 16 in the September in which they began the school, so most of her pupils would have applied in their last year of elementary school. While domestic service positions were dropping after the war, the need for good household training, cookery and household economy did not, so Hilda kept a steady stream of pupils through the school.

Her newspaper adverts were aimed at 'educated ladies, trained for home duties or as matrons, house mistresses, housekeepers, &c', and offered short courses in cookery, laundry, dressmaking, needlework and upholstery. Presumably, as dressmaking and needlework were Hilda's specialist subjects, the other staff members provided teaching on cookery and laundry and upholstery. The Wiltshire Council funding was ended completely in 1922, meaning that Hilda had to fund the school via other means.

The *Queen* magazine ran a feature on the school, which had by this time expanded to take in the house Ellandune next door, in October 1923, entitled 'Solving the domestic problem: training school for mistresses and maids'. This was reprinted in the *Wiltshire Times*. Hilda was interviewed as part of the article:

> Every girl of every class should be trained in housewifery and cookery… If mistresses were well trained, they would know how to direct their maids and would then know what to demand from them. In earlier days young women of the leisured classes learnt much of housekeeping and cookery in their own homes, but today for various reasons that is not the case, and consequently they should take a course of domestic training on

the completion of their ordinary education. Girls of the working classes should also, I think, be given such a course, for nowadays mistresses are not willing to take a completely untrained maid.

Though clearly steeped in the rigorous class system that was still prevalent in the 1920s, Hilda indicated through the piece that she believed all the attendees of the school – whatever their background – could learn from each other. There was considerable emphasis on the basics and principles of simple and plain cookery, with the ethos being that once the rudiments were mastered, more complicated and luxurious dishes were then possible. Care of household linens and delicate items was a particular focus of the laundry work, and during the course each girl was required to make in dressmaking classes a simple serge dress, a cotton dress, a blouse and a camisole, in order to gain different stitches and techniques. There was instruction in gardening too, and a continuation of reading and arithmetic, an hour of physical exercise ('drill') each day, and team games on the weekends. Though not academic, the training the students received would have been eminently valuable for the lives they were expected to lead in the 1920s and 1930s.

Away from the school, Hilda visited her brother Conran in Canada several times during the 1920s and 30s. She was also known locally around Trowbridge as someone who could be prevailed upon for good works in the community, and seems to have commanded a great deal of respect.

Though Hilda's domain no longer had council funding, the school still played a role in the discourse of domestic subject teaching for the entire county. Girls were offered places from across communities, and the teachers were part of conferences on related subjects that were sometimes held on the premises. Domestic subjects were gradually being further embedded into the curriculum being studied by girls and young women at the elementary schools, so they were seen as no less important in a full education, but the focus was gradually being changed to something everyone did – for example at Nelson Haden Girls' School – rather than being an add on. Nevertheless, the Wiltshire School of Cookery and Domestic Economy continued to offer scholarships to girls across Wiltshire.

The school also continued to operate into the Second World War, though it was found that examining students in cookery was difficult under rationing. Dressmaking, laundry and needlework were unaffected. Examination of these subjects was undertaken by Miss King, who had been Hilda's employer at the Bath Domestic School before the First World War.

The Butler Education Act of 1944, however, sounded the death knell for the school. This, in addition to raising the school leaving age to 15 which would have taken a good portion of Hilda's pupils away, established Secondary Modern schools – which were aimed at taking on a great deal of the vocational study provision, and would place domestic subjects into their buildings. The Trowbridge Technical School absorbed their provision. The school was formally closed in 1945, and Hilda retired after 26 years in charge.

She advertised for, and found, a local home for herself and a female companion – Clarissa Taylor, her school deputy and close friend – from the end of term in July 1945. They set up residence in Hilperton, just outside Trowbridge. The former school buildings became a temporary hostel for children attending the Bath Technical College and the Trowbridge Technical School, and later the Ethandune Girls' Hostel.

One of the roles that Hilda had held during her tenure as principle of the Wiltshire Cookery School was President of the Trowbridge Local Association of Girl Guides, and she continued that into her retirement. She also sat on the Hilperton Parish Council.

She died in December 1952, aged 71, and her funeral took place at Hilperton, and chief mourners were her widowed sister Muriel and her close friend Clarissa. Her former bosses – Katherine Willson and Miss King of the Bath Domestic College – also attended the service. Probate, of over £5,000, was granted to her sister and a married friend.

Hilda's subjects are still taught in British schools, but under different monikers to those which she knew. They were known as domestic science or home science in the 1960s and 70s, as some of the drive towards labour saving and scientific gains were applied to the home and into the comprehensive school system. This had evolved into a subject called home economics being taught to all pupils regardless of gender in the 1980s, alongside a variant of a subject called craft, design and technology. Today, pupils study design and technology with a focus on food and nutrition, or with a focus on textiles. Household economy is not touched upon. Neither is laundry work.

References

Aberdeen Press and Journal, 27 July 1904, Huntly School Board
Architects of Victorian Manchester, The Girls Institute Mill Street Ancoats Manchester, at https://manchestervictorianarchitects.org.uk/buildings/the-girls-institute-mill-street-ancoats-manchester (accessed 3.1.2025)
Bath Chronicle and Weekly Gazette, 10 June 1897, Wiltshire School of Cookery
Bath Chronicle and Weekly Gazette, 30 March 1899, Wiltshire School of Cookery
Bath Chronicle and Weekly Gazette, 24 May 1906, Wilts School of Cookery
The Bath Directory, 1894, p.708
Bristol Times and Mirror, 24 March 1904, Wiltshire School of Cookery
Canada, Incoming Passenger Lists, 1865-1935, held by Ancestry.co.uk
Devizes and Wiltshire Gazette, 31 August 1905, Wiltshire School of Cookery and Domestic Economy, Trowbridge
Devizes and Wilts Advertiser, 7 October 1909, The Wiltshire School of Cookery and Domestic Economy: To be continued at Trowbridge
Devizes and Wilts Advertiser, 24 February 1916, Pocket Money for Children
Devizes and Wilts Advertiser, 19 October 1916, Wilts Domestic School: The Contemplated Closing
Devizes and Wilts Advertiser, 7 June 1917, Wilts County Council: Scholarships for Domestic Training
England and Wales, National Probate Calendar (Index of Wills and Administrations), 1858-1995, held by Ancestry.co.uk
England and Wales Indexes of Births, Marriages and Deaths, held by Ancestry.co.uk
Folkestone, Hythe, Sandgate & Cheriton Herald, 7 March 1908, School of Cookery
Folkestone, Hythe, Sandgate & Cheriton Herald, 9 January 1909, School of Cookery
Folkestone, Hythe, Sandgate & Cheriton Herald, 9 April 1910, School of Cookery
Folkestone, Hythe, Sandgate & Cheriton Herald, 8 April 1911, School of Cookery
Kelly's Directory of Manchester, 1895
Manchester Courier, 13 November 1886, Deaths
Manchester Courier, 17 December 1894, The Manchester School Board Institutes for Women and Girls
Manchester Courier, 8 September 1905, Gorton Technical Teaching
Manchester, England, Non-Conformist Births and Baptisms, 1758-1912, held by Ancestry.co.uk
Marlborough Times, 2 May 1891, County School of Cookery For Wiltshire
Marlborough Times, 26 November 1892, The Wiltshire School of Cookery
Marlborough Times, 10 June 1893, To Elementary School Teachers
Marlborough Times, 23 May 1896, The Wiltshire School of Cookery
McGregor, G (1987) The Red Books of Scotland. Volume 5
North Wilts Herald, 5 April 1929, Wilts Domestic Economy School, Trowbridge
Salisbury Times, 7 September 1894, Wiltshire School of Cookery
Salisbury Times, 1 December 1905, The Cookery Classes

Salisbury Times, 20 October 1905, Teachers of Domestic Science
Salisbury Times, 24 December 1909, County Cookery School: New Quarters and New Constitution
The Scotsman, 23 June 1924, Death of Sir James Shaw Hay
Scotland 1921 census, held by Scotlandspeople.co.uk
Scotland, National Probate Index (Calendar of Confirmations and Inventories), 1876-1936, held by Ancestry.co.uk
Swindon Advertiser, 4 November 1905, Wilts School of Cookery
Swindon Advertiser, 30 May 1913, Wilts County Council. Scholarships for Domestic Training
Teachers' Registration Council Registers 1914-1948, held by Findmypast.co.uk
Trowbridge Chronicle, 25 March 1893, Wiltshire School of Cookery and Domestic Economy
Trowbridge Chronicle, 14 March 1903, Wiltshire School of Cookery
Trowbridge Chronicle, 8 October 1904, School of Cookery and Domestic Economy
Trowbridge Chronicle, 19 August 1905, Wiltshire School of Cookery and Domestic Economy Trowbridge
UK Census collection, held by Ancestry.co.uk
UK and Ireland, Incoming Passenger Lists, 1878-1960, held by Ancestry.co.uk
Votes for Women, 26 August 1910, Wiltshire School of Domestic Economy
Warminster Herald, 14 May 1892, Cookery
Warminster & Westbury journal, and Wilts County Advertiser, 23 December 1893, Wiltshire School of Cookery and Domestic Economy
Western Gazette, 7 August 1908, Cookery Appointment
Wellington Journal, 15 June 1907, Scholastic Appointment
Wiltshire Telegraph, 24 December 1904, County School of Cookery: Presentations to Miss Bridgman
Wiltshire Telegraph, 5 June 1909, The Wiltshire School of Cookery: Proposed removal to Salisbury
Wiltshire Times and Trowbridge Advertiser, 19 May 1894, Educational
Wiltshire Times and Trowbridge Advertiser, 2 September 1905, Wiltshire School of Cookery and Domestic Economy, Trowbridge
Wiltshire Times and Trowbridge Advertiser, 5 January 1907, Wilts School of Cookery, Trowbridge
Wiltshire Times and Trowbridge Advertiser, 2 November 1907, Appointment
Wiltshire Times and Trowbridge Advertiser, 23 July 1910, Training in Domestic Economy
Wiltshire Times and Trowbridge Advertiser, 18 March 1911, Educational
Wiltshire Times and Trowbridge Advertiser, 13 November 1915, Trowbridge. Gathering of Teachers: Domestic Economy and the War
Wiltshire Times and Trowbridge Advertiser, 28 April 1917, Food Economy
Wiltshire Times and Trowbridge Advertiser, 28 June 1919, Wilts County Council: Scholarships for Domestic Training
Wiltshire Times and Trowbridge Advertiser, 29 April 1922, The Wiltshire School of Cookery and Domestic Economy, Trowbridge
Wiltshire Times and Trowbridge Advertiser, 27 January 1923, The Wiltshire School

of Cookery, Domestic Economy and Needlework
Wiltshire Times and Trowbridge Advertiser, 20 October 1923, Solving the Domestic Problem: A Training School for Mistresses and Maids
Wiltshire Times and Trowbridge Advertiser, 26 May 1928, Teachers of Domestic Economy
Wiltshire Times and Trowbridge Advertiser, 24 November 1928, Conference of Domestic Teachers
Wiltshire Times and Trowbridge Advertiser, 29 September 1934, Trowbridge
Wiltshire Times and Trowbridge Advertiser, 15 December 1934, The Wiltshire School of Cookery and Domestic Economy, Trowbridge
Wiltshire Times and Trowbridge Advertiser, 13 November 1937, The Wiltshire School of Cookery and Domestic Science, Trowbridge
Wiltshire Times and Trowbridge Advertiser, 6 December 1941, School of Domestic Science
Wiltshire Times and Trowbridge Advertiser, 4 November 1944, Poppy Day. Cookery Demonstration and Concert
Wiltshire Times and Trowbridge Advertiser, 31 March 1945, School of Domestic Science
Wiltshire Times and Trowbridge Advertiser, 12 May 1945, Wanted, an Unfurnished House
Wiltshire Times and Trowbridge Advertiser, 2 June 1945, Domestic Science School
Wiltshire Times and Trowbridge Advertiser, 4 August 1945, Domestic Science Teaching
Wiltshire Times and Trowbridge Advertiser, 6 October 1945, Hilperton Road Hostel
Wiltshire Times and Trowbridge Advertiser, 27 December 1952, Miss L H Hay

Christian Hamilton

Dog breeding, and displaying, was often a women's field – invariably practised in the early days by those with country interests of hunting, shooting and fishing, as many gentry with big houses kept hounds – but it became a realm where women could carve their own hierarchy as these newer ideas had never before been the preserve of men.

The popularity of pedigree dog displaying, with prizes awarded for skill and stature, really began in the 1880s, with the first Crufts dog show to feature all breeds occurring at the Royal Agricultural Hall, Islington, in 1891.

It was at this event that Christian – a breeder of Pomeranians and kennel owner from Seend – came to prominence, and remained a well-known figure in that world for many years.

Her unusual first name, today more commonly given to boys, was inherited from her paternal grandmother, and like this relative was followed by the second name Anne – so she was probably called Christian Anne or Christianne for much of her life. She was born in Edinburgh into an exceedingly prominent Scottish family in August 1861, the daughter of Alexander Hamilton, a commander in the Royal Navy and his wife Mary Moorhouse Walters, herself a daughter of a solicitor. Their marriage in 1857, and Christian's birth, were announced in the newspapers of the day.

The family initially resided in her father's family's mansion house, Rozelle in Ayrshire, an extensive estate on the southern coast of Scotland which has the cottage where Robert Burns was born within its original bounds.

The first glimpse of the family on the 1871 census at Rozelle shows that Christian – then aged 9 – was the only child, and their household had a full complement of servants. There was a waiting maid, several housemaids, a laundress, a cook, a dairymaid and a kitchenmaid. This speaks of an extremely comfortable existence, with a great deal of wealth. Christian's father's family had made a small fortune in the 18th century by investing in tobacco and sugar in the West Indies. Rozelle House is now an art gallery and museum run by South Ayrshire Council, and has operated as such since the late 1960s when the ensuing Hamilton family fell on harder times. Rozelle was a language corruption of La Rochelle, in France, where the Hamilton family had previously done business.

At some point after 1871, the family left Scotland. Christian's father Alexander, who was a good 20 years older than her mother, suffered an illness and was advised to move to a warmer climate for the good of his health. They picked Penzance in Cornwall, practically as far south as it is possible to get on the English mainland, and took up residence in the town's Clarence House – another grand and large property. This house is today a centre for yoga and holistic therapies, and at some point was also a school. Christian would likely have been educated there and earlier at Rozelle by a governess.

It was here, in early 1881, that Christian's father died, aged 65. His remains were sent up to Ayrshire for burial, but Christian and her mother remained resident in Cornwall. Christian would have then been 20. She and her mother inherited well over £4,000 – a fortune by Victorian standards – and still drew investment income from the estate in Scotland. Their household in Penzance had four servants – mostly waiting staff, and a coachman – and Christian's mother Mary also took in two locally-born nieces to the house, to bring them up too. They also later took in a nephew, born in Ireland and a few years younger than Christian, who became their companion.

Whether this acquisition of relatives was in part Mary's frustrated desire to have more children, or an act of extreme kindness to less fortunate family, is open to question. But Christian also had an adopted sister at some point over the next few years. Caroline Corrie was the daughter of the paymaster in the Royal Navy, so the family was probably known to the family through Christian's father's work. Her parents appear to have split up – partly due to a very public row over her father's wish to sell her mother's inherited property – and while her two older siblings remained with their mother, Caroline lived with Christian and her mother and was given on census returns as an adopted daughter.

The family's move to Seend – a large-ish village between Melksham and Devizes – appears to have happened around 1883. The house that Christian, Mary and their entourage moved into was the village manor house. This had been the family property of the prominent Awdry family for much of its history – a family who were later to produce Wilbert Vere Awdry, the author of *Thomas The Tank Engine*. However, some financial issues meant that most of that family had preferred to live at Notton, nearer Chippenham, so Seend Manor had been being let to tenants since 1852.

The previous tenant was John William Montagu, a retired admiral from the Royal Navy, who had lived there with two of his daughters. He died there in late 1882. It's possible that the naval connection may have passed through to Christian and Mary to alert them to the property being available, as they were definitely the next residents and probably arrived in the months after Montagu's death.

The Seend Manor they moved into was the second house on the High Street site. Ambrose Awdry II had bought the site in 1695 and built a 'mansion house' before 1701, but this had been rebuilt by Ambrose Awdry IV in 1767 and it was extended at some point in the 19th century. Christian and Mary's household had many rooms and several outbuildings as well as extensive gardens. Today, the building is Grade II* listed.

It was from Seend that Christian really established her kennels, which cemented her as a dog breeder of note. She housed her dogs in a former stable at the manor, which was divided into pens with bedding and exercise space, and kept the temperature constant. She also took great care with the diet and feeding of her dogs. A feature on her in *The Gentlewoman* reported that smaller dogs had minced mutton with vegetables and bread, while the larger ones had houndmeal, porridge, soaked biscuits and meat scraps.

The first dog of note from Christian's kennel, which she called Rozelle after her father's Scottish estate, was Garda Boo Wooh who was winning awards in 1887. She was then handler of a collie called Shirley, owned by Mr A.H. Megson, at three dog shows in London in 1889. She bought Shirley from him later that year.

At the inaugural Crufts dog show and competition in 1891, her Pomeranian dog won the class and she was elected the first president of the Pomeranian Club – a position she held for many years. Her champion Pomeranians, and the first two to win under Kennel Club rules, were Rob of Rozelle and Konig of Rozelle, both white dogs which were Christian's speciality. It is likely that Christian and her competing dogs took the train from Seend, which had a station, up to London for these shows.

Pomeranians were also the favourite dogs of Queen Victoria, and her dogs would often rival canines from the royal kennel at many dog shows.

Pugs, greyhounds and Great Bernards were also favourites of Christian, and all featured in her Rozelle kennel. She also was renowned for her horses – though these were more her mother's speciality – and kept cattle, pigs, poultry and cats. In addition, she was active in the local hunt, as many women of her class and background were.

She and her mother Mary were resident at Seend Manor until at least 1895, as she recommended a health tonic for dogs and cats in a newspaper advert from that property. Her mother recommended horse tonics in the same advert. Round about that time her adoptive sister Caroline reached the age of 18, and left their care, traveling to New York – probably to visit her mother. She later made a good marriage.

An author, Charles Henry Lane, wrote about Christian in his 1895 book *Dog Shows and Doggy People*, when they were living at Seend Manor.

> Miss Hamilton is not one of those exhibitors who take a languid interest in their pets. On almost every occasion she attends the shows, and very frequently takes her dogs into the rings; and only those who, like the writer, have very often had her dogs before them can appreciate the courtesy with which she invariably receives the awards, whether favourable to her pets or not, so that I have often thought that, in a wide experience of all classes of exhibitors, from Royalty to the humblest among working men and women, I have never met a better loser than the subject of this slight sketch, who, I need hardly say, enjoys the regard of a large circle of

friends, and, from her generous support of shows in general and amiable disposition, is universally popular in all assemblies of Doggy People, and year after year has been re-elected President of the Pomeranian Club.

She was well known for attending the dog shows with her charges – which sounds as if others in her position would perhaps send a worker instead – and her mother would also attend too if possible. However, by this stage her mother's favourite hobby was collecting exotic birds. Seend Manor must have seemed like a menagerie between all the animals kept within its walls.

Toy Pomeranians became a favourite for Christian to breed, a class of the dog kept under seven pounds in weight and encouraged by the Pomeranian Club. These required a special diet and care, of which Christian was an authority.

The piece on her in *The Gentlewoman* in June 1895 describes one of her dogs.

> 'Sensation of Rozelle' is a lovely little white dog, weighing under 7lbs, with a profuse, pure white coat, long, foxy head, ears erect and not too far apart, and a perfectly black nose. A white Pomeranian so small with very nearly perfect points is a great rarity, the majority of them being much too large for lapdogs.

At some point between 1895 and the spring of 1901, Christian and Mary gave up the manor at Seend – another wealthy naval widow moved in with her son – and moved to another large property. This was Bannerdown House in Batheaston, just outside Bath. They still had two of Christian's cousins with them, and several servants. The Rozelle kennel, and all of Christian's animals and interests moved with them. From here she continued to breed and exhibit her dogs, and also sold eggs from her chickens.

There are adverts in newspapers in the early 20th century for the Bannerdown household hiring servants. Often these are for strong women, as the work would have involved a good deal of mucking out and cleaning after committed countrywomen. They also specify that their employees must all be church attenders. The adverts reveal that the household kept four women servants, and occasionally a lad to manage the garden. They ate dinner late, and sent out their washing to a steam laundry.

Her mother Mary died at the beginning of 1904, and was buried alongside her husband in Ayrshire. Christian, who had never married, continued to live in the large property outside Bath with her animals and servants. She kept up the presidency of the Pomeranian society position for many years.

The 1911 census has her at Bannerdown, supporting herself by private means – probably invested inheritance. She had a housekeeper, and a home help, along with a cook, two housemaids and a between maid. All would probably have been involved in the care of her dogs and other animals, to a greater or lesser extent.

Christian died in June 1918, aged 57, and was cremated and her remains sent to Ayrshire. No family appears to have attended her funeral – the house coachman was in appearance, as were solicitors. Her house contents sold at auction that autumn, and included various fancy furniture – a mahogany dining set, a fine pianoforte, several dozen bottles of wine, a dinner gong – alongside four pedigree Pomeranian dogs, ponies, cobs and a horse.

References

Bath Chronicle and Weekly Gazette, 6 July 1918, The Late Miss Hamilton
Bath Chronicle and Weekly Gazette, 28 September 1918, The Estate of the late Miss Hamilton, deceased
Caledonian Mercury, 29 June 1857, Marriages
Clarence House Therapy Centre, (2023) Therapy centre for the community, at https://www.clarencehousetherapycentre.co.uk/ (accessed 12.1.2025)
Clifton Society, 14 March 1901, Clifton Society Talk
Clifton Society, 3 March 1904, Deaths
Clifton Society, 3 March 1904, Bath
Cornishman, 13 January 1881, Penzance
Crufts: The Kennel Club, (2025,) History, at https://crufts.org.uk/about-us/history/ (accessed 12.1.2025)
England and Wales Census Collection, held by Ancestry.co.uk
England & Wales, National Probate Calendar (Index of Wills and Administrations), 1858-1995, held by Ancestry.co.uk
Field, 16 February 1895, Pacita for Grease
Gentlewoman, 15 June 1895, Our Pet Dog Gallery
Historical Environment Scotland (1987), Rozelle (La Rochelle), at https://portal.historicenvironment.scot/apex/f?p=1505:300:::::VIEWTYPE,VIEWREF:designation,GDL00335 (accessed 12.1.2025)
Lane, C.H. (1902), *Dog shows and doggy people*, Hutchinson & Co, London

Naval & Military Gazette and Weekly Chronicle of the United Service, 31 August 1861, Births

Peterson, V (2008), *German Spitz and Pomeranian Project* at https://www.pomeranianproject.com/1860--1915 (accessed 11.1.2025)

Scotland, National Probate Index (Calendar of Confirmations and Inventories), 1876-1936, held by Ancestry.co.uk

Scotland, Select Births and Baptisms, 1564-1950, held by Ancestry.co.uk

South Ayrshire Council, (2024) Remembrance Woodland at Rozelle Park, at https://www.ballantrae.org.uk/places-to-visit/listing/rozelle-house-maclaurin-galleries-ayr/ (accessed 12.1.2025)

Western Daily Press, 3 December 1917, Farming and Gardening

Western Gazette, 31 July 1903, Cook Wanted

Western Gazette, 17 February 1905, Girls Wanted

Western Gazette, 18 September 1908, Lad wanted

Westminster, London, England, Church of England Marriages and Banns, 1754-1935, held by Ancestry.co.uk

Wiltshire Times and Trowbridge Advertiser, 8 June 1907, Girl (strong) wanted

Wiltshire Times and Trowbridge Advertiser, 8 March 1913, For sale

Helen and Grace Bagnall

SISTERS HELEN AND Grace Bagnall, the eldest and second youngest of five girls, were both involved in women's suffrage, and both teachers – and therefore it is difficult at times, since both were unmarried and known as Miss Bagnall, to separate their activities.

They came from a moneyed family that moved around as their iron master father's business dictated – Helen Maurice Bagnall was born in Pattingham, Staffordshire in 1860 while Grace Mackworth Bagnall's birth occurred in Whitby, Yorkshire in 1867, and their sisters were born in places in between. The family also spent time in Northamptonshire, Bedfordshire, and London while they were growing up. Their father Thomas Bagnall ran Grosmont Iron Works, just outside Whitby, with his brother Charles – who was at one time MP for Whitby. As could be expected from an employer of 300 men, the sisters were brought up in big houses with full complements of servants and educated by governesses.

Both went on to be teachers in girls' schools – Helen first, as she was the elder, in the early 1880s when she was in her early 20s, and Grace followed in her footsteps in the 1890s. Their other two unmarried sisters, Jessie and Alice, remained with their parents, while the youngest – Gertrude – married a Reverend Perkins.

Both Helen and Grace held long positions at prestigious private girls' schools. Helen was among the first staff members at the Worcester High School for Girls, later named the Alice Ottley School after its founding headteacher (and Helen's great friend), for over 18 years. Alice Ottley was a committed educationalist, and the sister-in-law of May Ottley who was featured in *Extraordinary Ordinary Women ... of North Wiltshire*. That school merged with the Royal Grammar School in 2007 and has now dropped her name.

Grace – after a start as a science and biology teacher in Berkshire, and a turn as a teacher at Oxford Girls' High School – had a position at The Godolphin School in Salisbury for 21 years which began in 1895.

Godolphin School was over 100 years old already when she joined the staff, and the fact that Grace was a science teacher shows the progressive girls' education being offered by these schools at this time, as it was very much considered a subject just for the boys in this era. She was part of the staff presided over by seminal headteacher Mary Alice Douglas, who compiled and wrote a bicentennial history of the school in the 1920s.

Both Helen and Grace were form tutors, taking charge of older girls, and both held the second in command position – effectively the deputy head – in her school. Grace's subject at Godolphin was nominally history, but she also was involved in other subjects, including 'contemporary studies', which appears to have been reading the newspapers aloud and discussing their content while darning and mending, and played the double bass in the school orchestra.

A pupil from the 1890s describes the scene in Godolphin school's bicentennial celebration book:

> 'Contemporary,' went on on mending nights. I'm not sure whether it did not tend to stop supervision of darning, but the exponent of the news has been grateful ever since for having been obliged to be such a diligent student of the news of the day. Miss Edwards always had an eye for telling articles and for pictures. As the houses grew in number, the Contemporary news-tellers were multiplied, and Miss Grace Bagnall was drawn in.
>
> Miss Grace Bagnall. Is there any need to describe her? Can't you all see her? And can't you hear her quiet, emphatic and compelling words of command in St. Margaret's field? Her grave, if sometimes severe, face broke into frequent smiles all over it, and if Miss Bagnall didn't understand a joke, who did?

In 1904, however, Helen chose to leave her job in Worcester and took a job at a newly established school in New Zealand – the Diocesan High School for Girls in Auckland. The idea was that she would bring her experience and her school's values to this new school. The journey, which went via Australia, would have taken weeks at sea at this time, and she travelled as a missionary. It's known, from shipping records, that she made this journey at least twice over the next few years.

This teaching position in New Zealand may have been the catalyst for Helen's involvement in women's suffrage, although by her very background – she was of wealthy stock, unmarried, and very educated

– she was ripe to take on the fight even before she left the UK. Women in New Zealand gained the vote in 1893, with various states in Australia also granting it around the time Helen went over, and she would have been there to see the political and social gains that were made by newly enfranchised women. She even voted herself, she revealed later.

The right for women to vote in New Zealand was won after a seven-year campaign and 13 petitions which were presented to their parliament. This led to the Electoral Act 1893, which gave all adult women in the country the right to vote. 109,461 women enrolled to vote in the 1893 election. And by the time Helen arrived this had been the norm for over ten years.

The Diocesan High School for Girls was a private Anglican foundation, a project of the Bishop of Auckland, and as such would have upheld church and British educational values in a setting far removed from their source. It formally opened in May 1904. Helen would have been on the first school staff, under headteacher Mary Etheldred Pulling and her assistant Beatrice Ward, who had also emigrated from the UK. The school revered the work of Alice Ottley's school at Worcester, and Helen's background there. There were initially 25 pupils, but the school soon expanded from its initial two classrooms to a cluster of buildings with a school hall, and began taking in boarders in 1905. As time went on, and Mary Pulling grew to know more about New Zealand, she pulled the school more towards the ideals of the country at its best and away from the British values of its founding. School magazines, published monthly, show Helen deeply embedded in the life of the school.

Helen left the school and returned to the UK in 1909. She wrote back to the school – girls and mistresses alike – after a meet up of Worcester High School old girls, and her thoughts on both being home and the need for teachers in the further reaches of the British empire were published in the *Diocesan High School Chronicle*.

> Since I have come back I have heard a good deal about the dearth of teachers for Indian and Colonial posts. There seem to be always a large number of schools urgently needing really good teachers, some with good salaries, others offering only a maintenance, but they wait and wait, and the work suffers awfully, and no one will go. Teachers are so absorbed in their work at home, that the cry from these struggling outposts of the Church does not stir them...

I can assure anyone, from my own experience, that they would gain enormously by a spell of 'imperial service.' The widening of interests, the new friends, new scenes, new outlook; the sense of youth and vigour and hope which one imbibes in a new country; the feeling in your bones that the British Empire is a reality; and not mere 'words, words, words,' but a huge responsibility; and that England is, after all, rather a small part of it, while at the same time - she has been the maker of its history; these are a few of the advantages you get by living for a few years far enough away to see things in perspective. You learn, too, what really matters in life, and what is only convention or opinion; what you can do without, even in Church privileges, and what you must hold on to for your very life, as it is your Life.

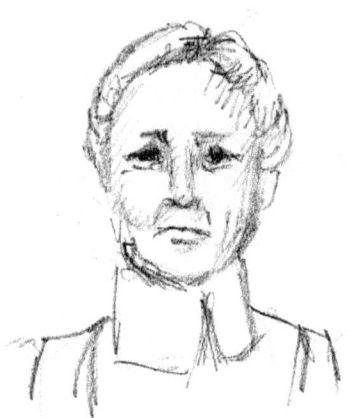

Rather than returning to Worcester, Helen took up a job at Godolphin School – where Grace was still teaching, in Salisbury – although her unmarried and unemployed sisters were now based around Bristol and Bath and she could have gone to live with them had she wanted. She took up a position as the school's senior English teacher, and was described on her entry to the school as headteacher Mary Alice Douglas's dearest and first proper friend. They had met while both were teaching in Worcester. Other members of the Bagnall family were also instrumental in the life of the school. Their reverend brother-in-law gave religious addresses to the girls of Godolphin School, and their middle sister was responsible for some of the wood carving in the school hall.

Helen remained in position for around 18 months, then travelled back again to New Zealand's Diocesan High School for Girls to teach there for a further year. She went via Cape Town in South Africa, and sent a letter back to Godolphin school describing her experiences there from a point in the Southern Ocean, which was published in the school magazine. She was at Diocesan for the coronation of King George V, and took an active part in the school's celebrations, affirming New Zealand's links with the UK.

She returned to the UK for good in 1912, as her father was dying, coming via Palestine. She didn't quite make it before he passed, however. She then began teaching at Godolphin again, and was also in charge of a newly-established housewifery course. In the early part of the First World War, Helen was involved in helping the influx of Belgian refugees fleeing the conflict.

And, while Grace was the deputy head, it was Helen who gave the address to Godolphin School on Empire Day in May 1916, mentioning the war effort and pride in their country.

The teachers at Godolphin were quite politically active. In 1915 several of them – including Helen and the headmistress – were instrumental in setting up a branch of the National Union of Women Workers in Salisbury, and inaugural meetings were held at the school. The aim of the organisation was to co-ordinate the voluntary efforts of women across Great Britain. The school group was keen for women to become police officers, and to that end was instrumental in setting up women's patrols to help police the streets of Salisbury. Grace was part of the women's patrols, alongside fellow mistress Florence Mildred White – who went on to become the first documented British policewoman, in the Salisbury force, in 1918 – and they would tramp the streets rain or shine.

Another achievement of this union – of which Helen was the honorary secretary – was the setting up of the Hulse Clinic in Mill Road, Salisbury, in 1915 to offer new thinking in maternity services, taking care of mothers and new babies, and therefore cut infant deaths. The high rate of infant death in the UK at this time (172.13 per thousand births in 1910, falling to 162.78 by 1915) was particularly tied to the suffrage movement, as it was felt that cutting it – by educating women in better health practices and greater moral fortitude (faith still being a huge part of life at this time) would also improve the day-to-day lives of women alongside their eventual enfranchisement. The building was acquired in the memory of guards' officer Edward Hulse, son of Sir Edward Hulse – a former MP of Salisbury – and his wife Lady Edith. Soldier Edward had been killed in the Great War, and his memorial house was also the headquarters of the Y.W.C.A. for Salisbury.

It is known that the headteacher of Godolphin School at the time, Mary Alice Douglas, was a suffrage sympathiser. However, it appears that it was Helen – possibly with Grace – who was directly involved in the fight to gain women the vote. Salisbury had a history of being on the non-direct-action suffragist side of the campaign, on account of its links to the leader of the National Union of Women's Suffrage Societies (NUWSS) Millicent Fawcett, whose husband – prominent MP Henry Fawcett – came from the town. Despite this being his birthplace, he represented both Brighton and Hackney in Parliament, but after his death in 1884 a statue was erected to him in Salisbury marketplace.

Millicent Fawcett was also not a resident of the city in her later years, but retained the family connection through her suffrage work. Salisbury had a NUWSS branch from 1909, which was joined in 1913 by a South Wiltshire branch. By June 1914 Helen Bagnall was the chairwoman of the Salisbury Women's Suffrage Society, and over the next few years was writing to correct claims made by anti-suffragists from that position in the pro-suffrage *The Common Cause* newspaper. Her refutations were backed up with statistics from Australia, which indicate that she was well versed in her subject.

The *Common Cause* reported, on Friday 15 May 1914:

> At an Anti-suffrage meeting held in the Assembly Rooms at Salisbury, on May 5th, several mis-statements were made by Mrs Gladstone Solomon of such importance that we reproduce a correction of them by Miss Helen Bagnall, of the Salisbury Society within the N.U.W.S.S., which appeared in the *Salisbury and Winchester Journal* of May 9th: -
>
> 'SIR, - May I venture to call the attention of Anti-suffragists among your readers to one or two mis-statements which were made about matters of fact by the speakers who addressed their meeting this week?
>
> Since the grant of the vote to women the birth-rate in the Australian Commonwealth has risen, not fallen, as Mrs. Gladstone Solomon thought and asserted in answer to a question. The Commonwealth enfranchised women in 1902. In 1911 the birth-rate – 27.1 per thousand – was the highest for ten years; and in 1912 it was 28.65 per thousand.

The next statement was rather 'tall', even for America. We were told that since women have had the vote in California they have brought in 4,000 Bills and passed 1,200 of them. Now, women were enfranchised there only in 1911, so they must, indeed, have been hard at work! To find the number of Bills produced per diem would be a pretty little exercise in arithmetic. And do the Californian women electors really bring in Bills? Even men electors here cannot quite do that.

My third point does not touch a mis-statement such as setting aside a truth in relation to a great national problem. Mrs Solomon was deploring, as we all do, the high infant death rate in England, and she attributed it to the ignorance of mothers, as, again, we all must do to a great extent. But when asked whether the British Medical Association had not asserted the waste of infant life is also, and very largely, due to the prevalence of vice, she contemptuously dismissed this opinion, and raised a laugh by saying that 'doctors are not always right', and said that her view was that of Mr. Parr, of the Prevention of Cruelty to Children Society, thus setting his lay opinion above that of the highest medical experts.

If, sir, the opposition which the Woman's Movement has to encounter from Anti-suffragists is supported by such rash mis-statements of fact, and by shutting the eyes to unwelcome truth, it cannot be very formidable.

Grace left teaching at Christmas 1916, feeling that her own home needed her. Presumably her two unmarried sisters, who had been supported by their parents while they had been alive, were part of that household.

Headteacher Mary Alice Douglas said in address at Grace's departure:

> ...the loss is very great, whether I think of her as she has been these last three years, Second Mistress in the School, and thinking and caring about the whole work, and taking my place so ably and faithfully; or whether I think: of her as the friend and helper of all the other members of the Staff; or as a very important part of the life of St. Margaret's or as the Form Mistress of the Upper and Lower VI.; or as teacher of History to so man),; or as one who makes each girl here, little or big, feel her responsibility with regard to punctuality and order; or, finally, as playing the Double Bass in the Orchestra. But of one thing we may be sure, that

no particle of good work and purpose is ever wasted, or ever dies, and so we are not going to feel that Miss Bagnall's good work is going to stop. That would be a very poor way of showing our gratitude to her. No, her leaving us is a call to us to try and carry on every good thing here that she has cared about. And now the School is longing to show their feelings for her in the usual way, and I know the Governors of the School will be the first to lead in a demonstration of the usual character.

Helen took up her position as deputy head, and continued to teach at the school until the spring term of 1919. She lent her garden for school play performances in the summer of 1917.

Some women (only those over thirty, or owning property that qualified) in the UK gained the vote in February 1918, and by this stage one of the Miss Bagnalls – almost certainly Helen – was chair of the Salisbury and South Wilts Women's Suffrage Society. As the general election was announced at the end of that year, she chaired a meeting of the society supported by Alys Russell (separated wife of philosopher Bertrand Russell, and a key political suffrage speaker in her own right), where they read out answers on women's political issues that the society had put to both candidates. Miss Bagnall also spoke:

(She) commented on the approaching election, and said that women were privileged to help to put into power men, and, she hoped with all her heart, some women who had to undertake the largest and heaviest task ever laid upon statesmen since the world began. The task before the Parliament and the Government was to make a peace which would endure, to end war for ever by a League of Nations that would last, and, secondly, to build up a new England, and make it, as Mr Lloyd George said last week, 'A country fit for heroes to live in, and for their wives and children to live in.' Having made the world, by this victory, safe for democracy, they now had to make democracy safe from selfishness and pride. The old political weapons completely failed to accomplish either of these tasks – they failed to keep the peace of the world, and failed to build up an England that they could live in. New forces were needed. Could women bring into the electorate a new spirit instead of the party spirit – a spirit of unity, without suspicion, spite, slander and the imputing of evil motives to these who did not think exactly as they did, but crediting those from whom they differed with common honesty and with really holding the opinions they professed? Could women not also, as was being done in other countries, help to make politics a clean thing, and selling of votes which often meant the selling of souls. Let them stand for clean hands.

By 1921, Helen was the divinity mistress at Wycombe Abbey Public School for Girls in Buckinghamshire. That school, a private boarding school for girls, was founded in 1896 by Dame Frances Dove. Grace had retired from teaching completely, and was living with her sisters Jessie and Alice in Painswick, Gloucestershire.

The gaining of the vote for women saw the gradual disbandment of Women's Suffrage Societies, although true equality was pushed for by all parties with a stake in the game until it was granted in 1928. Helen contributed to Mary Alice Douglas's bicentenary book on the Godolphin School in 1926, and both sisters often attended the yearly commemoration ceremony held at the school and other alumni events. Helen also attended a gathering of old girls from the New Zealand Diocesan High School for Girls in the early 1930s, and would actively send her news back to the school.

Both Helen and Grace retired to a house – Ivythorpe – at Freshford, near Bath, with their unmarried sisters – who were given the roles of cook and gardener – and lived out their last years in the quiet village. During the Second World War, the sisters provided a home to their niece, daughter of their youngest sister Gertrude, whose husband was stationed abroad with the RAF. Their niece had three small children – two boys and a girl – at the time, and they brought a great deal of life to the household. Helen mentioned these children in letters back to Diocesan High School for Girls throughout the war.

Both women died in the 1950s – Grace first, at 84 in 1952, and Helen two years later in 1954 at 94. Her death occurred at a house in Market Lavington, near Devizes, which may have been somewhere providing sheltered accommodation or elderly medical care at that time. Both women left decent sums of money to their remaining sisters.

References

Bedfordshire Mercury, 12 January 1912 Thomas Bagnall
Cambridge Independent Press, 14 May 1859 Marriages
Common Cause, 15 May 1914 Anti-suffragists' mis-statements at Salisbury
Common Cause, 29 May 1914 A Reply to Miss Bagnall
Common Cause, 5 June 1914 Anti-suffragist statements

Common Cause, 30 March 1917 Donations to N.U.W.S.S. Scottish Women's Hospital

Diocesan School for Girls, April Chronicle (1907) The Drilling Challenge Shield

Diocesan School for Girls, November Chronicle (1907) School House Girls' Notes

Diocesan School for Girls, December Chronicle (1908) Selwyn House Chronicle

Diocesan School for Girls, November Chronicle (1909) Our Contemporaries

Diocesan School for Girls, December Chronicle (1911) Hands Across The Sea

Diocesan School for Girls, December Chronicle (1914) Staff Notes

Diocesan School for Girls, Chronicle (1936) Staff Notes

Diocesan School for Girls, Chronicle (1943) Overseas

Diocesan School for Girls, Chronicle (1945) Overseas

Douglas, M.A. (1928) *The Godolphin School 1726-1926*, Longmans

England & Wales, 1921 census, held by Findmypast.co.uk

England & Wales, Civil Registration Birth Index, 1837-1915, held by Ancestry.co.uk

England & Wales, Civil Registration Death Index, 1916-2007, held by Ancestry.co.uk

England & Wales, National Probate Calendar (Index of Wills and Administrations), 1858-1995, held by Ancestry.co.uk

Gloucestershire, England, Electoral Registers, 1832-1974, held by Ancestry.co.uk

Godolphin School diary, 1908-1910, held by Wiltshire and Swindon History Centre

Godolphin School diary, 1912-1913, held by Wiltshire and Swindon History Centre

Godolphin School diary, 1926-1928, held by Wiltshire and Swindon History Centre

Godolphin WW1: Miss Bagnall, at https://web.archive.org/web/20190312055648/https://godolphinww1.com/tag/miss-bagnall/ (accessed 28.7.2024)

Hercock, F (1996). 'Pulling, Mary Etheldred', *Dictionary of New Zealand Biography*, at https://teara.govt.nz/en/biographies/3p36/pulling-mary-etheldred (accessed 29 July 2024)

Index To Register Of Passport Applications 1851-1903, held by Ancestry.co.uk

Loftus Advertiser, 28 November 1891 Grosmont

Ministry for Women, Women's Suffrage in Aotearoa New Zealand, at https://www.women.govt.nz/about-us/history-womens-suffrage-aotearoa-new-zealand (accessed 28.7.2024)

Morning Post, 8 April 1862, Births

Northamptonshire, England, Church of England Baptisms, 1813-1912, held by Ancestry.co.uk

North Yorkshire, England, Church of England Births and Baptisms, 1813-1921, held by Ancestry.co.uk

Passenger Lists Leaving UK 1890-1960, held by Findmypast.co.uk

Salisbury and Winchester Journal, 29 October 1910 Women's suffrage

Salisbury and Winchester Journal, 19 April 1913 Women and the suffrage

Salisbury and Winchester Journal, 25 April 1914 An Anti-Suffrage Meeting
Salisbury and Winchester Journal, 9 May 1914 The Woman's Suffrage Question
Salisbury and Winchester Journal, 30 May 1914 Anti Suffrage Meeting at Salisbury
Salisbury and Winchester Journal, 20 March 1915 Suffragists and the war
Salisbury and Winchester Journal, 28 August 1915 The Serbian Hospital Fund
Salisbury Times, 6 December 1918, Women and the Election
Staffordshire, England, Church of England Births and Baptisms, 1813-1900, held by Ancestry.co.uk
Teacher's Registration Council Registers 1914-1948, held by Findmypast.co.uk
UK and Ireland, Outward Passenger Lists, 1890-1960, held by Ancestry.co.uk
UK Census Collection, held by Ancestry.co.uk
Whitby Gazette, 5 April 1862 Grosmont
Whitby Gazette, 26 December 1863 Grosmont
Whitby Gazette, 26 September 1885 Grosmont
Whitby Gazette, 7 February 1890 Whitby
Whitby Gazette, 19 January 1900 Death of Mrs Charles Bagnall
Worcestershire Chronicle, 8 July 1893 The Worcester High School
Yorkshire Evening Press, 16 January 1889 Whitby District
Yorkshire Post and Leeds Intelligencer, 6 January 1912 Obituary: Mr Thomas Bagnall

West Lavington Ladies' Football Team of 1920

THE BANNING OF women footballers by the FA in 1921 has, quite rightly, been written about widely.

Despite the fact that women had been regularly playing football since the 1880s, and this had increased tenfold over the First World War years, this prohibition effectively banned the women's game from being played at the professional grounds and pitches of clubs affiliated to The FA. The FA Consultative Committee's resolution stated:

> Complaints having been made as to football being played by women, Council felt impelled to express the strong opinion that the game of football is quite unsuitable for females and should not be encouraged. Complaints have also been made as to the conditions under which some

of the matches have been arranged and played, and the appropriation of receipts to other than charitable objects. The Council are further of the opinion that an excessive proportion of the receipts are absorbed in expenses and an inadequate percentage devoted to charitable objects.

For these reasons the Council requests the Clubs belonging to the Association refuse the use of their grounds for such matches.

This meant that, in theory, the women's amateur game could continue outside of FA spaces – on village greens or other common land – but the idea that football was unsuitable for women trickled down into all levels of the sport. And skilful players like the well-known Lily Parr, of Preston's Dick, Kerr Ladies Football Club, were virtually ignored until the ban was lifted in 1971. And many years beyond that too, with blatant sexism in support and coverage of women's football still heard regularly in the 21st century.

It's against this background that a particularly joyful photograph of the West Lavington Ladies' Football Team of 1920 has survived, acting as proof that women were not only playing the game but enjoying it in Wiltshire in the run up to the FA ban. There is no newspaper report of the result, nor which position they all played, but the names of the six a-side team that played in a local fete that year have also been handed down with the image: Marjorie Ross, Lottie Fielding, Eva Collins, Nancy Barer, May Draper and Maud Wright. Though not necessarily in that order in the image, from left to right, all in tightly laced boots with a heavy leather ball.

After the FA ruling the following year, and the change in general attitude towards the women's game, these six – despite not being professional club players and their charitable matches probably being slim on the ground – may not ever have played together as a team again, but at least one of them cared enough to keep the image and remember their names.

The obvious candidate for the person who preserved the photograph for posterity is 'Nancy Barer', who appears to have been badly rendered from the name Amelia Borer – Nancy was perhaps her nickname. In 1939 she was the caretaker of the Lavington Sports Club, and as such perhaps best placed to care for memories of past sporting glories.

Nancy, aka Amelia Teasdale Borer, was born in 1894, so would have been 26 when the West Lavington team photo was taken. She was a baker's daughter, and had come from Littleton Panell, just north of West Lavington. She was one of four children, but had lost her only brother William early, when he died following a seizure in 1908. Her sister Lilian was known as Jenny, and her sister Olive was known as Joe, so it is no surprise that Amelia was widely known as Nancy.

As a master baker, Nancy's father John seems to have been financially comfortable enough for her not to have to work – though she undoubtedly probably did help out in the business through her childhood and young adulthood. She is given as not in work or education on the 1911 census, aged 17, so was probably deeply immersed in the life of the village. A report of a concert given by the Primrose League in West Lavington in April 1914 gives her as a pianist accompanying performing vocalists.

Her sister Jenny married in 1911 and moved away to Sturminster in Dorset. Her sister Joe married a farrier turned soldier in 1915, and stayed in West Lavington for a few years, eventually moving to Hampshire when her husband became a jockey, and then emigrating to New Zealand in the 1920s.

Nancy did not marry, however, and the 1921 census – a year after the football team photo – finds her assisting her father with his baking business. She may have been of the generation who lost a sweetheart in the Great War, or she may have been more focused on supporting her parents as the last child at home. She may also not have been inclined to marry.

Her father died the following year, aged 62. Nancy and her mother may have continued his business in some way, but she was not an official baker by any capacity, so they may have had to look for other sources of income. Her mother Elizabeth died at the end of the 1920s.

There's no further document reference to Nancy until the 1939 register, taken in September that year. She was at this stage the caretaker of West Lavington Sports Club, and living alone in a bungalow next to the club, probably on the edge of the sports pitches. Much of that job would have been caring for the club facilities and pitches, but she may also have been able to kick a ball around if she was so inclined. Ironically, as the ground was part of the FA, she would have been looking after male footballers but unable to play herself.

Nancy finally did get married in 1943, to Lindo Pike – who ran the local newsagents and was about ten years her junior. She would have been around 49 years old. She was widowed in 1951, and seems to have moved into Devizes during her final years. She lived at the geriatric hospital, St James', and died there in 1978.

The first name in the list of the West Lavington players, 'local school teacher' Marjorie Ross, is another candidate for who may have just held on to the team photograph and its information.

She was Florence Marjorie Ross, and was born in Charlwood in Surrey at the end of 1903, arriving in West Lavington around 1916 via Clapcott in Berkshire. Her father Joseph was a head gardener, probably for teams that worked the large ornamental gardens around bigger houses, and seems to have taken his family to various locations for work. This means that Marjorie, though remembered as a local school teacher on the football team photo caption, would have been 16 when the picture was taken.

She's described as a school mistress on the 1921 census, at the age of 17 and a half. As such, she is unlikely to have completed any fully formal training as a teacher as she was a little on the young side, but was probably employed in the local elementary school to work with the very youngest pupils as she built her experience. There's a report of a Market Lavington Schools Football tournament having taken place in 1924, in the *Wiltshire Times and Trowbridge Advertiser*, so it is perhaps feasible that she had some hand in organising this contest, even if she was no longer allowed to play herself.

As she was remembered as a local school teacher, she must have remained at the school for a long while, to have been able to make an impression on the generations of children passing through her classroom, and she probably had formal teacher training at Salisbury as her career progressed.

Her father Joseph, who had worked as head gardener for Lord Justice Warrington at Clyffe Hall in Littleton Pannell, died in 1926. Under the marriage bar for women teachers she would have had to resign her job if she'd wanted to marry, so she either didn't have the opportunity or loved her job too much to give it up.

Her elder sister Ella, who worked as a postal clerk, didn't marry either as she was subject to similar restrictions. She worked in Richmond Upon Thames and Esher in Surrey, and died in 1951. Like Marjorie, younger brother Stanley went into education, teaching woodwork, and eventually taught at Harefield near Uxbridge. He didn't marry either. None of Marjorie's siblings stayed in the area, so she taught in the school and lived with her widowed mother.

Marjorie and her mother moved out of West Lavington at some point in the 1930s, and into a place on the High Street in nearby Devizes. She likely travelled back to the village school every day to teach. Her mother died in 1965.

Though the marriage bar was ended for women teachers (outside the London School Boards, which was earlier) with the 1944 Education act, Marjorie seems to have been of a traditional mindset. She finally married at the point of her retirement in 1968, to John Parr. John was a little older than her, and came from Poole in Dorset, where they lived together until his death in 1973. Marjorie then returned to West Lavington, and lived at Dauntsey House, a care home, until her death in 1982.

Aside from those who most likely preserved the photo, the other four women on the 1920 football team were all equally embedded in their community and the times that surrounded them.

Lottie Fielding, who came from nearby Worton, was born in May 1906, so was barely 14 when the photograph was taken, and was likely one of the two youngsters pictured on chairs to the far left or right. Her father, John Fielding, was a market gardener and farmer at West Winterslow when Lottie was small, and there's a report of their house – Maisey's Farm – being completely gutted by fire in July 1908 when Lottie was two. The house seems to have been either rebuilt or the family found alternative accommodation, as by the time of the 1911 census the family were still ensconced in West Winterslow. This census reveals that Lottie was the youngest child of nine, though two had died young, and her older siblings were assisting their parents on the farm.

In 1917, the family moved to Newgate Farm in West Lavington, which is where Lottie was living when she played for the women's football team at the summer 1920 fete. A year later, on the 1921 census, Lottie was 15 and living at home, with no occupation – save probably helping out on the farm but uncredited with that.

In 1927, shortly after Lottie's father had been taken to court for arrears regarding his farming business (and being liable for the debts of one of Lottie's brothers, who had absconded), Lottie married Alfred Moore in her home parish. She would have been 21 years old.

Alfred had been born in Newport in South Wales, and had served in the marines briefly, towards the end of the First World War. They had four children – one in West Lavington, two in the Amesbury area, and one in Salisbury – over the next decade, and by the outbreak of war were living in Amesbury on Alfred's wage as a stable lad.

Lottie was widowed in 1958, and Alfred was buried at Tilshead on Salisbury Plain. She married again the following year, to Clifford Potter. He had grown up in West Lavington too, and had worked as a labourer locally. She was his second wife, and gained stepchildren. Clifford was buried beside his first wife in Tilshead in 1961.

Lottie lived on until 1983, and died in the Salisbury area.

Eva Collins was the oldest of the 1920 team, probably the older woman standing to the right of the shot, and the only one who was married at the time the matches were played. Originally Eva Mahalia Ricketts, she'd been born in Dorset in 1881, to Saul – a labourer and sawyer – and his wife Julia. She grew up in Wimborne and Bournemouth, and was working as a housemaid by the time she was 20. She married labourer Albert James Collins in Wimborne in 1910, and by the following year they had settled together in Littleton Pannell – where Albert was from. Their son Albert Ralph was born in 1912.

This means that not only was Eva the only married member of the football team, she was also the only one of them who was a mother. There were no further children – which may have been down to Albert's service in the Hampshire Regiment in the First World War.

Albert became the local postman for the community, and Eva seems to have mostly stayed at home. Their son became a carpenter. Albert predeceased Eva in 1958, and she passed on in 1974.

May Draper, the fifth team member, was actually Elsie May Draper. She was, like Nancy, from Littleton Pannell, and one of ten children of a road man. Born in 1902, she'd have been 18 at the time of the photo being taken, and had lost her father Edward or Edwin (records don't quite agree) five years earlier.

At the time of the football team, her widowed mother Ruth was holding the family together in Littleton Panell, with the finances provided by May's older brothers, one of whom at least had served in the First World War. May lived at home but did not appear to go out to work.

In 1933, when she was around 31, she married Francis Matthews in the West Lavington area. He was a sawyer, working with wood machines. They didn't have any children together, and were living in Little Langford in the Wylye valley by the outbreak of the Second World War. She died in 1975 in the same area, but her husband lived until 1992.

The sixth and final member of the team was Maud Wright, who had been born in West London, to Frederick Wright – the manager of a brewery store – and his Trowbridge-born wife Rhoda. Maud and her five older siblings had landed in Market Lavington by 1911.

Her father signed up for service in the First World War, in the 4th Battalion of the Wiltshire Regiment, but died of cirrhosis of the liver shortly after being discharged in June 1915. Her mother then raised Maud and her older sister Gladys on her father's military pension.

Maud would have been about 17 when she played for West Lavington Ladies, and this seems to have been one of her last recorded events in the village. By the time of the 1921 census, a year later, she and sister Gladys were back in London. At 18 and a half, she had a job as a clerk with a tyre company, while Gladys was working as a typist for the same firm.

And, while her mother moved in with Maud's older brother Derek and his wife in Melksham, there's no further obvious record of Maud anywhere – and she probably married in London at some point over the 1920s and 1930s.

Nancy Borer, Marjorie Ross, Eva Collins, Lottie Fielding, May Draper, Maud Wright. The West Lavington Ladies six-a-side football team for one summer, possibly even just one day, in 1920. One of them probably played in goal. Another would have been a striker. Another concentrating more on defence. It probably wasn't a very important match in the scheme of things. We don't know who they played against in that fete, let alone what the score was.

But each of them looks joyful, and full of vim and vigour, so perhaps the photograph was taken after they won. And the spirit of optimism at that time for women, with many new openings available after the upheaval of the status quo caused by the First World War, assurances around work promised by David Lloyd George and the 1919 Sex Disqualification (Removal) Act (which in practice didn't materialise) and the newly given political opportunities is palpable from the image. The fact that within 18 months they'd be banned from continuing to play football when it was deemed not to be suitable for women, seems criminal.

References

1921 census of England and Wales, held by Findmypast.co.uk
Daniels, P (1999) *South Wiltshire* The History Press Ltd
Devizes and Wilts Advertiser, 19 March 1908, Sudden death
Devizes and Wilts Advertiser, 18 March 1909, In Memoriam

Devizes and Wilts Advertiser, 9 December 1915, Loe-Borer
England and Wales: Birth, Marriage and Death Records, held by Ancestry.co.uk
England & Wales, National Probate Calendar (Index of Wills and Administrations), 1858-1995, held by Ancestry.co.uk
North Wilts Herald, 23 December 1927, A Farmer's Failure: Statements at Public Examination. Son who disappeared.
Salisbury Times, 10 July 1908, House burnt down
UK census collection, held by Ancestry.co.uk
UK, British Army World War I Service Records, 1914-1920, held by Ancestry.co.uk
UK, British Army World War I Pension Records, 1914-1920, held by Ancestry.co.uk
Williamson, D. J. (1991). *Belles of the Ball* R&D Associates
Wiltshire, England, Church of England Births and Baptisms, 1813-1922, held by Ancestry.co.uk
Wiltshire, England, Church of England Marriages and Banns, 1754-1916, held by Ancestry.co.uk
Wiltshire, England, Church of England Deaths and Burials, 1813-1922 held by Ancestry.co.uk
Wiltshire Telegraph, 13 May 1911, Vincent-Borer
Wiltshire Telegraph, 18 April 1914, Primrose League
Wiltshire Times and Trowbridge Advertiser, 14 June 1924, Market Lavington Schools Football Tournament
Wiltshire Times and Trowbridge Advertiser, 17 July 1926, Market Lavington. Funeral of Mr Joseph Ross

Elise Possart or Hassan

THE ACT OF doing the washing, and keeping clothes and household linens clean, has invariably fallen to women, and the Victorian idea that cleanliness is next to Godliness just heaped extra pressure on those performing unpaid work in the home. However, the view that washing was 'women's work' inadvertently became a liberating idea for women in the later 19th and earlier 20th centuries. Industrial steam laundries, mechanising the washing and drying process, sprang up across the country – and in Wiltshire there was one each in Swindon, Chippenham, Devizes, Ludgershall, Warminster and Salisbury – all providing a steady stream of accessible jobs for women. These women-friendly businesses, though often dangerous with their processes, encouraged and normalised women in industrial settings. Laundries, cloth factories and food processing plants were all employing women to some degree, but this wasn't being repeated in bacon factories or flour mills or tanneries, or metal-based manufacturing.

Against this background, Warminster's Castle Steam Laundry, which opened in 1903, became the domain of Polish-born Elise Hassan – who was manageress at the helm for more than twenty years. Born in 1857, and of educated stock, the death of her father and then of her husband put her into the right place to become part of the first tranche of manageresses of any industrial business – at these steam laundries. And the idea that women could be managers may not have been as showy a liberating act as active suffrage in this period, but it was equally important to opening doors.

She'd arrived in the UK as Ernestine Franciska Elise Possart, at some point between 1861 and 1865 – when she would have been between the ages of five and nine. She was the eldest of four, and her family initially settled in South Wales after arriving from the continent. They came from a place they knew as Schlochau, which was at times in Prussia and other times in Germany – but now is known by its historic name Człuchów in modern day Poland.

Her father Gustav appears to have jumped onto the boom in international shipping around ports like Swansea and Cardiff – which were mostly exporting copper and coal respectively – and moved his family (Elise, plus her mother Theresa and siblings Maria, Ernst and Max) to the area in the early 1860s. However, the first definite record of Gustav in South Wales is his bankruptcy. He and another man, Carl Lobeck, had been running a ship chandlery and provision business in Swansea, and it had failed in the summer of 1865.

This would have plunged the family from a relatively well-off existence to a precarious one. Gustav would have been able to work, but could not have kept the money until his debts were paid off and his bankruptcy order lifted. Elise (who never went by the name Ernestine), as the oldest child, was around nine, which was occasionally employable in that era, but had very little earning potential. Her family's class status also would have meant that it would have been preferred for her not to work if at all possible.

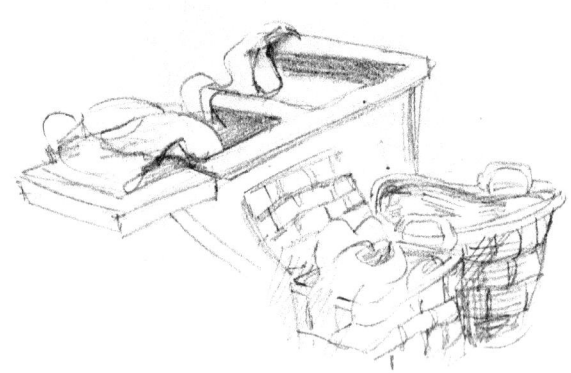

Things then seem to have gone from bad to worse. The family, who lodged in Loudon Square in Cardiff – a relatively genteel part of the city's very international Tiger Bay community, which grew around the docks and the export business – appears in the out-relief records for Cardiff workhouse in the later part of the 1860s. Gustav, described as 45 with a wife and four dependant children, was given as ill and destitute. He was given two pounds and sixteen shillings to get the family through eight weeks.

By the time we find Elise on the 1871 census, she was out of the household and working, probably due to necessity and claiming to be 18, which probably increased her possible wages. She was a servant to the family of shipkeeper – Edmund Crockford, who owned the Thisbe – and was moored up in Cardiff East Dock. Her duties would have been those of a normal domestic servant at the time, with cleaning, fetching and carrying, but with the added twist of being carried out aboard ship. The ship's chaplain and his wife, as well as Edmund Crockford, his wife and four children, were also aboard, and only employed Elise as help, so she would likely have been extremely busy in this role. Cardiff docks was an incredibly busy and crowded place at this time, crammed full of sailing ships that were loading and unloading cargo, and it was usually possible to cross the water by stepping from deck to deck. At times, it could also be quite a dangerous place, as health and safety wasn't a consideration.

At this time, the ship Thisbe was undergoing conversion to a church on a ship, aiming at salvation for the local population. Church services were held aboard several times a week, and there was a theological reading room below deck. This was the establishment in which Elise worked.

Her younger sister Maria had also found work to support the family, saying she was 16. She was a general servant too, but on dry land – for a ship's broker like her father, and in a house on Cardiff's North Church Street. Their parents and two youngest siblings were lodging back at Loudon Square, where Gustav had got himself back on his feet and was working as a merchant's clerk.

However, this reprieve was short-lived. Gustav made many more appearances in the Cardiff workhouse out relief records over the next few years, and had increasingly serious health problems. He was granted 27 weeks of relief in 1872 for paralysis, so was clearly unable to work. Later on, the relief – which was usually money – included a 3.5 lbs bag of cornmeal, so he was struggling to feed his family. As that decade moved on the relief, and his health issues, increased. There are longer stretches of the family being given help, and his condition becomes total paralysis.

The main core of the family moved from Loudon Square to Bute Road in 1873, which was a step downwards economically, and they would likely have still been renting. Throughout this period, his dependants fluctuate from three to two children, so Elise was probably working steadily elsewhere, and Maria too. The final entry in the workhouse series is in 1875, when the family are given one last piece of relief – for 20 weeks, but Gustav is noted as having died. Elise would have been around 18. Elise's mother Theresa does not appear to have received the same treatment, so they were on their own.

Two years later, in the autumn of 1877, Elise married George Hassan (sometimes Hassen) in Cardiff. She would have been around 20. Their marriage did not take place in an Anglican establishment, so would have been either at the registry office or one of the other smaller non-conformist churches around the area – like the Norwegian Church in Cardiff Bay, which served that immigrant community.

George does not feature in many records from Wales, or indeed England, and as such was probably not born in the UK either, but there's no census record available that tells us his birthplace. He was probably part of the international community in Tiger Bay, and as such could have his origins anywhere – as George could be an Anglicised version of any number of names. It is therefore harder to get a handle on their relationship, but we know from shipping records that he was a ship's steward – so probably working on boats leaving Cardiff and going back and forth across the Atlantic Ocean. This would have been a good and stable job, and probably have given Elise a better sense of security. Indeed, by the time the 1881 census was taken, four years later, she seems to have given up work and called herself a steward's wife. This may mean that she accompanied George on voyages, but it was more likely that she stayed and built their home while he was away.

The 1881 census finds her at home with her mother and younger brother Ernst at Ludlow Street in Cardiff, in the city's lower Riverside area and close to the water. Ernst, now Anglicised as Ernest, was supporting the family by working as an accountant's clerk – showing that the Possart children had all been well-educated. The other brother, Max, had recently married and moved around the corner. He also worked as a clerk, so had probably supported the family until his marriage.

Elise and George did not have any children. He seems to have continued working on the steam ships crossing the Atlantic, working as a steward, while there is no record of her on any crew list, so she probably stayed at home. Things could change in an instant for her though. In 1886 George was on the iron-hulled steamer Darlington, sailing from New Orleans to Bremen in Germany, when the captain didn't station a lookout as they were passing Bermuda. The boat crashed into the Western Reef, and capsized. The five officers and 23 crew were lucky, as all survived, and George was picked up by the boat Arizona. He was repatriated to Liverpool, and presumably back to Elise. Today, divers in Bermuda tour the wreck of the Darlington.

George survived that misadventure, but was not so lucky two years later. In February 1888 he was working on the boat Raphael, and was taken ill with heart disease. He was admitted to the civil hospital in Gibraltar, but died there. This made Elise a widow at the age of around 30. The fact that she had no children meant that she was free to decide what happened next, rather than having to provide for her dependants.

Elise's level of education and class background then came into play. As someone who was well educated and literate, with a middle-class background from both her family and that of her former husband, she was perfectly placed to take on the opportunity that then came her way. By 1891 she was the forewoman at a steam laundry close to her residence in Cardiff. The likely premises at that time was the South Wales Steam Laundry on the corner of Redlaver Street and Clive Road, which was a going concern by at least 1887.

The invention of technology to enable washing to be undertaken on an industrial scale revolutionised the position of working-class women in the workforce. Steam laundries began to spring up across many cities, and then in a smattering of market towns too. Whereas previously women were employed in some industrial processes – notably weaving and cloth making, glove making, and some food production factories – the advent of the steam laundry was a place almost entirely staffed by women. Laundry being generally considered 'women's work' meant that the handful of men they employed were either the owner, or the fireman in charge of the boiler (the work required a continual stream of hot water which needed to be kept going), or the carman who drove completed laundry orders to customers. Every other job on the premises went to women – sorting, washing, starching, rinsing, mangling, drying, ironing, folding and packing. Many bigger premises offered linens services for hotels and boarding houses, so sheets, pillowcases, tablecloths, napkins, and towels, in addition to clothes. And some would also clean curtains and blankets.

The South Wales Steam Laundry grew to offer many of these services, and had a stables, coach house and dwelling house at its rear. A couple of decades later, as immigrants from the Far East started to come further into Cardiff than the docks and Tiger Bay, many of these places were owned and run by people of Chinese origin – much like similar premises on the American seaboard. But, at the time Elise was forewoman, the staff of the laundry was generally drawn from those of a Welsh and English background from the local area. As forewoman, she would not have been directly in charge of the business, but instead oversaw all of the day-to-day operations and was responsible for keeping the work moving. Some of these places offered shift flexibility, to fit around other responsibilities. They were also generally more sympathetic about employing married women, and those with children.

The next logical step up the ladder for Elise was to be a manageress in one of these workplaces, and this she undertook around 1900. She moved away from Cardiff and up to London, settling for a time in Hammersmith. The likely premises that she managed here was the Royal Chiswick Laundry in British Grove in Chiswick, which wasn't far away from her home in Percy Street. This was one of the thirteen premises across the capital which had come together as a united business in 1897, and as manageress of a London premises, Elise would have increased her experience and prestige.

This laundry would have offered broadly similar services to the place she'd left behind in Cardiff. However, adverts of about that time boast that collars were a speciality, as this was in an era where formal shirt collars were detachable from the shirts, and often washed and starched separately. They were reattached to the garment by tiny buttons along the neckline. The laundry also offered a department for dyeing, cleaning and carpet beating by steam power, so was again an industrial step up from Cardiff. Elise can be found in Hammersmith, as a laundry manager, living on Percy Street on the 1901 census. She was in a divided dwelling, but employed a domestic servant so was bringing in a good wage.

By 1907, however, Elise had moved back closer to home and taken a laundry manageress position in Warminster in Wiltshire. This would have been about half the previous distance to home by train, and more convenient to travel back to Cardiff should the urge take her.

The Castle Steam Laundry in Warminster had opened in the autumn of 1903. It's impossible to tell if Elise was its first manageress, as she doesn't appear in a trade directory in that position until 1907, but if she wasn't the first woman to hold the job she was almost certainly the second. New laundries would recruit and tempt women away from established premises.

The building she now ran was owned by a gentleman elsewhere in the town, Mr Morrice, but she seems to have had total jurisdiction over the premises. The site, in George Street, had previously been a pub called The Castle, which gave the laundry its name. Today, the laundry building is long gone, and a set of sheltered accommodation apartments sit where it used to be.

On opening in November 1903, the *Warminster & Westbury journal, and Wilts County Advertiser* said:

> Years gone by it was customary to see the gentle sex standing ankle deep in water washing our household line in a tube of water and wood ashes – known as lye. They started their muslin wear with an extract of that well-known hedge plant, the Cuckoo Pint (arum maculatum), drying the clothes in the garden when weather permitted and in their bedrooms when it rained.
>
> But the old order of things has changed and a visit to the Castle Laundry impresses one most vividly with this fact. Steam, washing machines, hydro-extractors, India-rubber wringers, collar shirt ironers, body ironers, and gas irons, all tell of modern invention and constructive skill.

So advanced for the time was Elise's laundry, that washing, rinsing and bluing of garments were all done by the same machine. They also had a hydro-extractor, an early type of tumble drier, which was capable of revolving 1,000 times and removed water far quicker than a mangle. They starched using rice or maize powder, and even had a separate machine for washing and ironing shirt collars. The newspaper was particularly glowing about the upstairs ironing room, calling it spacious, light and healthy. They were also keen to point out that the premises and conditions complied with Factory Acts brought in by Parliament, which other workplaces in the town were falling foul of around this time.

And, of all this, Elise was queen. The chance to run this facility, rather than being a smaller cog in a big industrial set up across several sites in London must have been very tempting, as it gave her a degree of autonomy at work that was still incredibly rare for women.

By the summer of 1906, the laundry also offered bathing facilities on the premises. Since the process to produce hot water was done on an industrial scale, it was much simpler to draw a bath in the laundry facilities than it would be heating enough liquid either over the fire or in a domestic boiler in the home. So, Elise's laundry also offered the chance to come and take a bath. There were men's days, and women's days, and two different grades of service, each offered for a small amount of pennies. Other laundries also offered something similar.

On the 1911 census, Elise was living on the laundry premises. Her niece Mary, from one of her brothers, lived with her and was being educated nearby. The other brother was managing a rope and twine manufactory back in Cardiff, so – despite their shaky start in life – the siblings were making good.

Elise continued to be manageress of the laundry throughout the First World War, when the women's employment that the premises offered came into its own alongside the growing tide of women going out to work. Past 1915 though, her name is not listed as manageress in trade directories, and instead the laundry owners are listed as being in charge instead. Geoffrey W Morrice does not appear to have removed Elise from her post though, as she still calls herself the manageress on the 1921 census. Rather, he seems to take the credit for the success of the business for himself as owner, rather that Elise who was doing all the work on the ground. Away from work, one of her brothers died in 1915.

Adverts for 1920 and 1921 show that with the age of the motor car the business was doing a roaring trade in picking up laundry from around the district on a twice weekly rota. They also had a telephone in this period. They offered collections and deliveries in the same week in Trowbridge, Wylye Valley, Westbury, Bradford-on-Avon and Frome, as well as Warminster. They specialised in washing of blankets and woollens, and made pains to point out that all silks and delicate work were hand-washed carefully. The need for bathing facilities gradually died out as home boilers and water heating facilities became better on a domestic scale. Later adverts boast of softer water – most Wiltshire water tends towards the hard side – and softer soap, which would have made a difference with household linens on skin.

By the time of the 1921 census, Elise appeared to have moved out from the laundry premises and into a house round the corner in Church Street. Her sister Maria, who had never married, lived with her and kept the house for her. She also took on a couple of boarders – one of independent means, and the other working for the watchmakers in Warminster – and a domestic servant. She gave herself as 65 on this document, and must have been heading for retirement age.

Because the local trade directories give the owner of the Laundry in their listings, rather than the manageress, it is hard to pinpoint exactly when Elise gave up her job. It's likely it was some point in the 1920s. But she stayed in Warminster for the rest of her life, living with her sister Maria. The second of her brothers died in 1927, back in Cardiff.

She died in 1933, and was buried in the town's St Denys churchyard as Franciska Ernestine Elise Hassan, widow. Her executors included Mr Morrice, the manager of the laundry, and it is probable that he was a close friend as well as her employer.

References

1921 census of England and Wales, held by Findmypast.co.uk
Bermuda 100 Wreck Sites, The Darlington, at https://bermuda100.ucsd.edu/darlington/ (accessed 30.6.2024)
England and Wales: Birth, Marriage and Death Records, held by Ancestry.co.uk
Grangetown Local History Society, *Grangetown's Laundries*, Fact Sheet No. 10, at http://www.grangetownhistory.co.uk/grangefact12.pdf (accessed 30.6.2024)
Liverpool, England, Crew Lists 1861-1919, held by Ancestry.co.uk
London Evening Standard, 25 May 1908, The Royal Chiswick Laundry
Perry's Bankrupt Gazette, 2 September 1865, Lobeck
Somerset Standard, 18 May 1934, A lady writes to her laundry
St James Gazette, 3 June 1897, The London United Laundries
UK census collection, held by Ancestry.co.uk
Warminster & Westbury journal, and Wilts County Advertiser, 24 October 1903, The Castle Steam Laundry
Warminster & Westbury journal, and Wilts County Advertiser, 28 November 1903, Warminster's Latest Industry
Warminster & Westbury journal, and Wilts County Advertiser, 2 April 1904, The Castle Steam Laundry
Warminster & Westbury journal, and Wilts County Advertiser, 21 January 1905, Castle Laundry
Warminster & Westbury journal, and Wilts County Advertiser, 14 July 1906, Baths! Baths! Baths!
Warwick, The Library, Modern Records Centre, Laundry workers, at https://warwick.ac.uk/services/library/mrc/archives_online/digital/tradeboard/laundry/ (accessed 30.6.2024)
Wiltshire, England, Church of England Deaths and Burials, 1813-1916, held by Ancestry.co.uk
Wiltshire Times and Trowbridge Advertiser, 9 October 1920, A first class laundry
Wiltshire Times and Trowbridge Advertiser, 3 December 1921, Calling twice each week
Wiltshire Times and Trowbridge Advertiser, 2 January 1926, A really good family laundry
Workhouse Records, Cardiff, 1861-68, held by Ancestry.co.uk
Workhouse Records, Cardiff, 1872-76, held by Ancestry.co.uk

Emma Bown and Ann Freemantle, both later called Goodfellow

EMMA AND ANN both hid the births of their babies. Emma in 1861, and Ann in 1876.

It comes as a surprise to many that, while concealing the birth of a child is a criminal offence, concealing a pregnancy is not against the law. Pregnancy and birth are so naturally interlinked that legal terms, definitions and rules that mark them out as different from each other in the eyes of the law can often be a difficult mental leap.

The 19th century was an era of poor public health and high infant mortality, with many families losing at least one if not more of their children before the age of five. Still more babies were stillborn or died within the first moments of life. This was so common that it might give the impression that parents, and society in general, were more used to these situations than we are today to the point of being blasé. And perhaps that might have been the case statistically, but on an individual basis confusion reigned as to the exact procedure to follow if the worst was to happen at birth. Suspicion and rumour were rife in communities where people lived crammed in on top of one another, and everyone knew each other's business. With illegitimacy being so stigmatised, an unmarried mother could fall under extra suspicion as she might want to keep herself respectable.

Since 1861, and the establishment of Section 60 of the Offences Against the Person Act, it has been an offence for anyone to conceal the birth of a child in England and Wales and Northern Ireland.

The exact wording of Section 60 reads:

> 60 Concealing the Birth of a Child.
> If any Woman shall be delivered of a Child, every Person who shall, by any secret Disposition of the dead Body of the said Child, whether such Child died before, at, or after its Birth, endeavour to conceal the Birth thereof,

shall be guilty of a Misdemeanour, and being convicted thereof shall be liable, at the Discretion of the Court, to be imprisoned for any Term not exceeding Two Years, with or without Hard Labour: Provided that if any Person tried for the Murder of any Child shall be acquitted thereof, it shall be lawful for the Jury by whose Verdict such Person shall be acquitted to find, in case it shall so appear in Evidence, that the Child had recently been born, and that such Person did, by some secret Disposition of the dead Body of such Child, endeavour to conceal the Birth thereof, and thereupon the Court may pass such Sentence as if such Person had been convicted upon an Indictment for the Concealment of the Birth.

Since Emma's offence actually took place in September 1861, between this act receiving Royal Assent in August and commencing on 1 November, she was actually charged under older legislation – the Offences Against the Person Act 1828 – which was clear that this was a crime that could only be committed by unmarried mothers, and had been so since Lord Ellenborough's Act of 1803.

Since Emma was unmarried, this case applied when her actions were discovered. But by the time she came to trial six months later, the 1861 Act was fully in force.

Emma Bown was born in Downton, a village about six miles south of Salisbury, though her parents seem to have been living in Barford St Martin – a few miles to the west of Salisbury – when she was baptised.

For much of her childhood she appears to have lived at Alderbury, another south Wiltshire village, where her father Joseph was a relatively prosperous dairyman. He had previously been a yeoman farmer in Somerset too, but had decided to focus on dairy farming, so the family was generally of good standing. Emma was at least the fifth child in the family, and grew up alongside a clutch of sisters with a couple of older brothers. The family also had a household servant, and a dairy labourer boarded with them too.

She lost her mother, Eliza, in the autumn of 1852 when she was barely ten years old. The bringing up of the family probably then fell to her oldest sister Elizabeth, who was then around the age of 14, but there were many children in the family to be looked after, including a small baby.

By the 1861 census, taken on the 7th of April that year, the family was living in Lower Lane in Alderbury, and Emma was the oldest child at home. She was 18 and working as a dairymaid for her father, and probably already pregnant.

As ever with stories like these, the father of Emma's child is never mentioned once in the case. She may well have been ignorant of the mechanics and risks of sexual intercourse – many well brought up young women of this time were kept in the dark until the moment of marriage. Her child's father may not have been similarly ignorant. He may also not have been in a position to marry her, which was often the solution to pregnancy outside of wedlock.

Emma seems either not to have known what was happening to her, or not to have been in a position to tell anyone. In an era where a corset was a vital staple of women's dress, it would have been possible to bind her middle to hide the pregnancy for many months, though eagle-eyed neighbours clearly suspected what had been going on.

The first mention of what happened to her is a garbled report in the *Salisbury and Winchester Journal* in mid-late September 1861, with many changes of narrative due to typesetting errors, and – though cases of this nature were often slightly sensationalised in the details – it's possible to pick up the chain of events.

On 30th August Emma had gone to George Plaskett's shop in Redlynch, another village a few miles to the south of Alderbury, where she regularly bought goods. While she was there, she asked to go to use their privy, which was located in the garden. And she may have been there for an hour or so.

Around two weeks later, George Plaskett's sons Mark and Frank saw what they thought was a dead cat at the bottom of the privy hole, and made initial fruitless attempts to retrieve it. The 'cat' was eventually brought up by one of the sons, placed in the nearby ash hole, and a policeman called. The policeman correctly identified a deceased male baby, and called for local doctor Charles Girdlestone to examine the body – but he was unable to say whether the child was completely full term, and whether he'd been stillborn or had died since birth.

Via a paper trail, and witnesses remembering the chain of events, Emma was eventually identified as the possible mother of the baby. She denied it, but was examined by Dr Girdlestone and he found her to have recently given birth.

The case was occasionally reported as a possible infanticide, and sometimes as a concealment of birth. The case rested on whether Emma had given birth in Mr Plaskett's privy on the 30th of August, and had been too inexperienced to save the life of her son (or he'd been stillborn), or whether she'd given birth elsewhere on the 24th of August and had taken him to Redlynch a week later for the express purpose of depositing his remains there away from home.

Mr Plaskett's employee, Eliza Weeks, who had been making butter on the premises that day, favoured the latter explanation, and claimed that Emma had even mentioned a baby to her while there. Other witnesses seem to refute this, two of them married women who seem to have suspected what was going on for Emma. One said she'd requested some castor oil – which could have been for constipation if that's what she thought was going on, rather than labour – and had advised her to have a warm cup of tea and talk to her father.

Emma was formally accused of concealment of birth, but was

allowed bail while they waited for the next assize court session, possibly due to her health and her young age. Her family was probably in a position to pay any bail demand, had there been any.

Emma's assize court trial was held at Devizes, towards the end of March in 1862. Standing trial in the same session was another woman, Marina Cottle, a cook from Limpley Stoke who had been accused of the same concealment offence. Both cases were referred to the crown court, held a few days later at the beginning of April.

Marina Cottle was convicted, and received a nine-month prison sentence. As for Emma, the charges were read out, and it was ascertained that she was undefended. The prosecution read out their case, claiming that Emma had given birth on 24th August but had waited until 30th August to hide her son's remains. The judge, Mr Justice Byles, stopped the case immediately, saying that he'd read the entire case and had found nothing in it to indicate that Emma had attempted to dispose of the baby whatsoever. He instructed the jury to acquit her, and they duly found her not guilty.

Therefore, though it probably stained her reputation locally, Emma was not sent to prison and did not undergo the hard labour that the 1861 Offences Against the Person Act recommended in these cases (that requirement was removed in 1948, in a rare change of legislation).

Eighteen months later, Emma married John Goodfellow in her home village of Alderbury. The long gap between these events would seem to indicate that John was not the father of the son that she had lost in the summer of 1861. Instead, Emma had formed a new relationship. John Goodfellow was a coppice labourer, around her age, and the son of a local shepherd.

They had actually had a child together before the marriage took place – son George Sidney Goodfellow was born at the beginning of September 1863, but only lived for fifteen days. The couple were clearly going to be married, so his illegitimate birth seems to have been fudged a little in the church records. Their marriage does not appear to have taken place in the village church however, perhaps due to this birth and Emma's previous child, as there is not a record of it taking place there. They probably went to the nearest registry office to tie it all up legally.

They had a further son, Henry George Goodfellow, in the spring of 1865, and another – Charles in August 1867. Charles only lived for two days, however, but Henry George survived.

Emma by this stage was not very well at all. She'd been suffering from heart disease for a while, and then developed tuberculosis, which complicated matters. She succumbed to both in February 1868, aged just 25. Her son Henry initially went to London to be brought up by Emma's sister Eliza, while her husband John continued living on at Alderbury, before marrying again and moving away entirely to become a carter in Staffordshire. Henry joined him there and became a baker and later a carpenter.

By the time that Ann's case occurred, fifteen years after Emma's, the restrictions and rules of the Offences Against the Person Act 1861 were fully established and understood. Ann's story treads along far less defined lines than Emma's, however, and is far more shocking in detail – but still is worth dissemination.

Though Ann, who was born Ann Freemantle, was of a similar age to Emma – she was born just three years later, in 1845 – her experiences were that of a grown woman of 31 and a mother, and not an inexperienced teenager.

She grew up in Tisbury, a village in South Wiltshire about 13 miles west of Salisbury, and was the daughter of John Freemantle – a journeyman stonemason – and his wife Charlotte née Mould.

Her childhood in Tisbury seems to have been unremarkable, growing up alongside a clutch of siblings and going into service as soon as she was old enough to bring in a wage, apart from the fact that at some point the family converted from the Church of England to a non-conformist church. It's from this church – the independent church at Zion Hill in Tisbury – that Ann married Matthew Henry Goodfellow in March 1867. He was known as Harry. Although the surname is the same as Emma's husband John, and they ended up in the same area, they do not appear to have been close relations to each other. He originated from Codford, and was living in Fugglestone St Peter at the time of his marriage to Ann.

Known as Henry, he worked as an ostler at the Rose and Crown pub in Alderbury, taking care of customers' horses when they pulled up for the night or just for a drink. Ann gave birth to a son, John, in the winter of 1871, but there were no other children from the marriage.

Ann's brush with the law took place in the summer of 1876. She'd lost her father in 1874, and her mother in 1875, and by late 1875 her husband had been ill for months, weak and unable to do much for himself, let alone hold a job. They had moved away from Alderbury into Salisbury, probably in an attempt to gain some work. At some point during Harry's illness, she'd become acquainted with Obediah Hawes, who was working as a railway porter at Tisbury station – at a time when most communities, however small, had a station or halt to enable easy transport. Exactly when she and Obediah, who was widowed with a young daughter, became more than just acquaintances isn't known, but by the time Harry died on 15 January 1876, Ann was pregnant.

Later medical opinion surrounding the case decided that Harry would have been incapable of fathering a child at the crucial time, so Ann's baby was viewed by the world at large as illegitimate – despite being conceived when she was in a marriage – and she seems to have regarded him as such too.

Ann's labour seems to have begun at some point on Friday 7th

July. On Sunday 9th July, it was assumed, she had a little boy, but he had died and she hadn't quite known what to do. On Tuesday 11th July, his remains were found tied in a cloth, and in a pan of boiling water on the fire.

Even today, when we are far more aware of the impact of mental health, grief, and conditions like post-natal psychosis on mothers, her actions are shocking.

Ann's baby was relatively quickly discovered, as in close communities the pains and noises associated with labour are unmistakeable, and she had started appearing around the neighbourhood again without a baby. Police and doctors were called, and Ann was arrested.

Again, under the auspices of the Offences Against the Person Act 1861, the case rested on whether Ann had wilfully killed her son, or whether he'd died of natural causes and – aware that he was illegitimate (with all the societal baggage that came with that) – she hadn't quite worked out what to do next, either through grief or post-natal illness or sheer ignorance.

Witnesses were called to the inquest – the policemen who discovered the baby and arrested Ann, doctors offering expert opinions, and neighbours who had seen and spoken to Ann over the past few days. The story, with full lurid details, was reprinted in newspapers all over the country.

The neighbours seemed to think that Ann's son had only lived long enough to take one breath, and that she'd asked at least a couple of them to help bury him, but they had been unwilling to do so. The two doctors both believed that the baby – which they considered to be full term rather than born early – wasn't alive when he was placed in the saucepan, but could not agree on the available evidence whether he'd been stillborn or killed after birth. One believed one way and one the other. The policemen appeared stoical and matter-of-fact on the details.

At the end of the inquest, the jury decided that the child had been wilfully murdered, and that verdict was returned. Ann was committed for trial at the next assizes session in Winchester, which sat in early December.

At this trial, Ann pleaded not guilty of murder, but admitted that she had concealed the birth. Obediah Hawes, the father of Ann's baby, who was apparently in the belief that he was to marry Ann and claimed that banns had been read in Tisbury, had not been told that she was pregnant. They seem to have mostly communicated by letter. Part of Ann's defence was that she had been keeping the pregnancy from him, which is why she'd concealed it.

One of the doctors in the case was ill on the day, and therefore not able to be examined. The one who did appear was the man who believed that Ann had killed the child before placing him in the saucepan, but the judge seems to have given extra credence to the missing doctor's views in his absence.

On the basis of the evidence, the jury decided that Ann wasn't guilty of murder, but agreed that she had concealed the birth and should be sentenced accordingly. The judge said, while passing sentence, that:

This was one of the most revolting cases he had ever heard of, both with regard to a mother's feeling and also the general feeling of humanity. The manner of disposing of the body was such as to wean all sympathy for her. The jury had done right in treating the case as one of concealment of birth, but it was of such revolting character and shrouded with such suspicion that it was not a case in which leniency might be considered. He should not sentence her to the full measure (two years), considering that she had been in prison since July. She would have to be imprisoned for fifteen months with hard labour.

With the benefit of 150 years of advances in medicine, understanding of women's health and mental illness, and a less rigid and more compassionate society, it is possible – while still shocked at the idea of how Ann treated her dead son – to understand how she may have ended up in the mindset and place that led to her actions. There does not appear to have been anything calculated in what happened, and instead she comes across as partially confused by the situation and not knowing quite what to do about it. She received no help in dealing with the death of a child she'd carried for nine months, and indeed had another living child – her son John – to consider in the midst of this. She may have been too weak after birth and blood loss to wield a spade to enable a proper burial, and instead was trying to find a way to end the situation that her strength allowed for. Furthermore, post-natal depression or even post-natal psychosis may have contributed to what she chose to do, but neither condition was recognised or treated at this time.

She also will not have had any therapy or support surrounding her emotions and well-being following all these events. She would have been treated for any physical symptoms that remained from giving birth, but mentally she would have been left to sink or swim.

Ann's fifteen-month sentence was served at Devizes Prison, a purpose-built facility by the Kennet and Avon Canal. This had a laundry, which served for the hard labour prescribed for many of the women inmates, but she may also have walked a treadmill for hours or done other repetitive and exhausting menial tasks.

Obediah Hawes does not seem to have waited for her to be released, which would have taken place in the summer of 1878. By the time of the 1881 census, he was living with someone else, whom he married later in that decade, and had taken up residence in London with his daughter in tow.

Ann herself also appears to have gone to London after her release, finding a position as a servant for a lodging house keeper in Kensington. Considering how much national coverage her story had received, the crowded nature of London would have been a good place to bury herself, and a lodging house would have seen a steady stream of people who didn't ask many questions.

Her son John doesn't appear to have gone to London with her by this stage, and it's unclear who had custody of him while Ann was in prison. It was probably a relative, more likely of Ann's rather than her former husband Harry. He does turn up in London later however, working on the railway and raising a large family with his wife Emily.

Of Ann there is no further trace. She probably either married or took up with someone whose name she used, furthering herself from the notoriety of the shocking case of Ann Goodfellow that had made national headlines.

Had either Emma or Ann been a married woman, or at least married to the father of their child in Ann's case, society and the law might have treated them differently in these cases. Practically all the cases of this nature charged unmarried women or widows, despite the updating of the 1861 Act to ensure that anyone could be held responsible. This may have been left over from the previous legislation in terms of perception, but also could show a considerable bias. Married women, held up as the ideal state for a woman in society at the time, seem to have been viewed far less suspiciously should their child have died – though many undoubtedly did.

References

Davies D.S. (1937) Child-Killing in English Law. *Modern Law Review.* 1(3): 203-23

England, Select Births and Christenings 1538-1975, held by Ancestry.co.uk
England & Wales, Civil Registration Birth Index, 1837-1915, held by Ancestry.co.uk
England & Wales, Civil Registration Death Index, 1916-2007, held by Ancestry.co.uk
England and Wales, Civil Registration Marriage Index, 1837-1915, held by Ancestry.co.uk
England & Wales, Criminal Registers, 1791-1892, held by Ancestry.co.uk
Hampshire Advertiser, 28 September 1861, Concealment of Birth
London, England, Church of England Marriages and Banns, 1754-1940, held by Ancestry.co.uk
Milne, E. (2023), *Concealment of Birth: A Case for Repeal*, Durham Law School
Salisbury and Winchester Journal, 21 September 1861, Concealment of Birth
Salisbury Times, 15 July 1876, Horrible Charge of Child Murder
UK, Calendar of Prisoners, 1868-1929, held by Ancestry.co.uk
UK Census Collection, held by Ancestry.co.uk
Wiltshire County Mirror, 18 September 1861, Redlynch – Supposed infanticide
Wiltshire County Mirror, 2 April 1862, Crown Court Monday
Wiltshire County Mirror, 28 November 1876 Winter Assizes 1876
Wiltshire County Mirror, 5 December 1876, Alleged wilful murder at Salisbury
Wiltshire, England, Church of England Births and Baptisms, 1813-1922, held by Ancestry.co.uk
Wiltshire, England, Church of England Deaths and Burials, 1813-1922, held by Ancestry.co.uk
Wiltshire, England, Church of England Marriages and Banns, 1754-1916, held by Ancestry.co.uk
Wiltshire, England, Non-Conformist Baptisms, Marriages and Burials, 1704-1987, held by Ancestry.co.uk

Dorcas Clark or Pearce/Pierce

Dorcas's tale is that of a classic Cinderella rags-to-riches elevation, albeit with a particular Trowbridge flavour.

Originally a cloth worker in one or more of Trowbridge's 19th century woollen mills, she ended up marrying the mill owner in the 1870s, became part of the town's high society, and spent the rest of her life in one of the biggest, grandest houses – which even had a deer park. But, it appears, she needed some societal improvement to be able to take that place, and at the expense, perhaps, of alienating her birth family.

Born in November 1847, around the Shail's Lane or Conigre area of Trowbridge, Dorcas was the child of woollen spinner Samuel Pierce or Pearce (the name is spelt both ways in the records) and his second wife Eliza Purnell, who had married as widows around five years earlier. There were various older siblings, some of whom had been born when her father was working in Lullington, north of Frome, but by the time of her birth the family were firmly established again in Trowbridge – with both her parents and her older siblings employed in the various woollen mills. Her mother Eliza appears to have continued to work – often as a burler or cloth mender, who would have checked for defects in the cloth – even while breastfeeding and raising her young family, as there were several more children after Dorcas too.

Dorcas would have grown up long before education was compulsory, so would probably have had limited schooling. She may well have attended Sunday school, and had some instruction and literacy within the town's National School, at that point located in Back Street, but there was no obligation for her to do so, and her family's economic situation probably meant that every child needed to earn as soon as they were able. That said, when Dorcas appears on the 1861 census, at the age of 13, she was yet to have a profession listed so may still be learning.

She went to work in one of Trowbridge's mills as soon as she was able, though. There were known to have been about 14 woollen cloth mills in the town in 1850, though numbers fluctuated, so there was no shortage of work, even if it wasn't well paid. The nearest place to home on Conigre was perhaps the small unnamed establishment on Shail's Lane, behind the gas works, but the bigger Innox Mills, Studley Mills, Home Mills and Stone Mills, all on the River Biss, were also within easy walking distance. Further into the main town, in the opposite direction, there were also woollen mills at Silver Street and Duke Street. Dorcas, on the 1871 census, was given as a cloth mill worker, but there is no indication which establishment employed her, or what job she held at the mill.

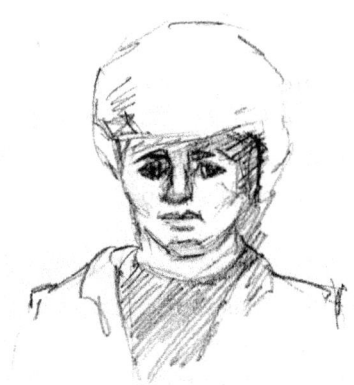

She may have been a burler, like her mother, but also could have been involved in weaving or spinning, packing or bailing cloth, carding raw fibre, piecing, winding, reeling or any number of other jobs. She may well have moved around the different mills as she grew older and her skill set increased. The one mill we know she definitely worked at, however, is the one her future husband owned.

Even this is hard to pinpoint exactly, as his family – the Clarks – were owners of several mills and firms in the town. In the middle of the 19th century, the firm of J and T Clark mostly ran Stone Mill, now located at the back of the Shires Shopping Centre, Duke Street Mill, and the vast Studley Mill on the opposite side of the river. In 1861 those premises consisted of an engine house and seven large mills with a power-loom shed.

J and T Clark were brothers John and Thomas Clark, who had been active clothiers in Trowbridge from the early 1800s onwards. Dorcas's eventual husband was Thomas's eldest son, also called Thomas, who was born in 1819 and thus nearly 30 years her senior. He had moved into Bellefield House (at the time of writing the home of Zircon Software, opposite the Ambulance Station on Hilperton Road) with his family in 1826 – after his uncle John Clark had bought it. On John Clark's death in 1846, ownership passed to his brother Thomas. Thomas Clark senior was given as a clothier on all five of his children's baptism records, and was clearly a massively respected presence in the town. When he died, in March 1859, most of the town's shops shut down as a mark of respect until his funeral procession had gone through the streets, and a newspaper report of the time called him a good master and an active magistrate.

On his death, the running of the mills owned by J and T Clark fell to his sons Thomas – later to marry Dorcas – William Perkins Clark and John Bayfield Clark. The Trowbridge cloth industry was booming in the latter half of the 19th century, with the benefits of the industrial revolution and increasing mechanisation in full swing. The difference in lifestyle between Thomas and Dorcas at this time was vast – while Dorcas was working long days at the mill for a pittance, Thomas erected a church – St Thomas's – to his parents' memory in 1870, at a cost of £7,000, around £705,000 in today's money.

However, things were beginning to change for Dorcas. She became deeply religious and had herself baptised into the Church of England as an adult, in 1865 (her parents did not to baptise any of their children at birth), and after the death of her mother Eliza in 1871, there are further differences. The 1871 census has her not at home with her widowed father and remaining siblings, as you might suspect, but instead lodging with an older woman annuitant – Sarah Peppler – on Charlotte Street. An annuitant was someone living off an inheritance, rather than having to work or receive poor relief, and in Sarah's case this was probably from her late husband, a cloth worker. It would not have been much, and Dorcas's lodging fee would have helped. But it also would have brought Dorcas into contact with different people.

It is unclear exactly when and how her relationship with Thomas began. He may well have met her during the course of her work at his mill, or through their church and shared Christian faith. He was now in his 50s, and – though busy with the business and his work as a Justice of the Peace, and being a Major with the Wiltshire Royal Volunteers – was probably regarded by the society surrounding him as a confirmed bachelor. Dorcas was in her twenties, and may have had prospects from young men around the district, but interest from a powerful mill owner should really have trumped anyone else that Trowbridge had to offer.

However it began, it appears that their romance could not continue without some changes. Dorcas was so far below Thomas's social station that the circles that he moved in might not have accepted her as an equal – despite all his money, background and influence. She was to 'marry up', and in some similar cases at this time, the partner from the lower of the social classes would shun their relatives, and exclude them from most of their lives following the marriage. It is unclear whether this happened in Dorcas's case though, but she was removed from the area and went to live at a rectory in Stanwick, Nottinghamshire, before the wedding could take place, and her father Samuel rehoused in better accommodation in Bath.

Being relocated to Nottinghamshire does not seem to have had any familial link to either Dorcas or Thomas. Rather, the move appears to have been to expose and familiarise Dorcas with the social mores of the class she was about to join, and a rectory would have been a good place to begin that process. Vicars were invariably from a gentry or monied background – the church was seen as a good career for a second or third son – as the higher education needed to qualify was prohibitive to anyone outside that circle. Thomas's cousin Joseph Clark was a vicar, and may have pulled a connection with the vicar in Stanwick, Nottinghamshire.

It isn't clear how long Dorcas spent there, but a newspaper report of her wedding from a Nottinghamshire publication says that she was highly respected and loved by the people of that area. She had been president of what was called the 'mother's meeting' – possibly something like today's Mother's Union in the Church of England. That organisation was founded in 1876, by Mary Sumner, who was wife of the rector of Old Alresford in Hampshire, and aimed to transform the home lives of families within the parish by helping the women to support each other in raising their children. Although Mary and Hampshire were a long way from Dorcas in Stanwick, it is possible that the parish she stayed in had similar ideas.

The newspaper also mentioned that she had run a Sunday School class on behalf of the parish, who had made a presentation to her of a silver thimble as a wedding gift, and such involvement in the life of the area indicates that she had perhaps been resident of Stanwick, staying with vicar Dr Mansfield and his family, for several months, if not years. There is even a possible mention of her in the parish from at least as early as the autumn of 1873, which would have meant a long separation from family and friends.

Her marriage to Thomas took place at Stanwick in October 1876, well out of the way of the Trowbridge people who might have wished her well. They were married by Thomas's cousin Joseph Clark, who was rector of Little Bytham in Lincolnshire. Her father is not given a mention in the wedding report whatsoever – he was either too infirm to travel the distance, or an unwelcome reminder of her background that was being left behind. She was given away by the vicar's son-in-law, rather than anyone from her family, and the wedding party was made up from her host's family. In addition to her father not being present, there is no mention of any of her numerous siblings. However, her dress – silk looped with orange blossom, and a tulle veil – is reported, as is a pre-wedding party held in the rectory's laundry room.

After the wedding, Dorcas – aged 29 – and Thomas – aged 57 and amazingly whiskered, according to a contemporary photograph – departed for a honeymoon on 'the continent', described as a wedding tour. This would probably have included Paris, which was a common destination for honeymooning couples in the 19th century, and visits to other places and sights that would have been totally out of reach for someone born into working in the Trowbridge woollen mills.

They were away for about three weeks, and were welcomed back to Trowbridge with great pomp and circumstance. The 2nd Wilts Rifle Corps, of which Thomas had formerly been the captain, the Wiltshire Volunteers and the staff of the Clark's mills banded together to bring Dorcas and Thomas home through the streets, pulling their carriage themselves rather than the horses that had been provided. The townspeople followed with torches, and a fife and drum band, and the church bells rang. At Bellefield they alighted, and the crowd dispersed.

And thus began Dorcas's life as the mistress of Bellefield. The three-storey house has flanking wings, a Bath stone front and Palladian windows, pleasure grounds and a six-acre walled paddock which the Clark family used as a deer park. It was originally built by another clothier – Julius Samuel Rich – in 1792, but he sold up to Edward Horlock Mortimer in 1798, and it was Mortimer's widow who had sold the property to the Clark family in the 1820s. This was a far cry from Dorcas's roots in the workers' cottages near the mills.

They do not appear to have had any children together. However, the Clark family was big, and many of Thomas's siblings and cousins had progeny, so she seems to have been known as Auntie Dorcas to many of them. A niece, Kate Pollard, daughter of one of Thomas's sisters, lived with them at Bellefield.

As mistress of this domain, she would have hired and managed the domestic servants for the house. There are several advertisements in the local newspapers for house parlourmaids and a 'good plain cook', simple food and a lack of strong flavours being part of a Victorian religious idea that this would bring you closer to God and therefore heaven at your demise, which the upper classes took very seriously. There were four servants in the household on the 1891 census, all of them domestic. Dorcas would also have kept up considerable involvement in the church, entertained guests and attended events on behalf of her husband's business. She may also have done some charity work for local organisations, in the company of other high society wives from the district. Aside from her more official duties, Dorcas was known to be a good embroiderer and would donate pieces as prizes and gifts.

Whether she was encouraged to eschew her family background or not, when her father died in 1882 – having returned to Trowbridge from his Bath residence – a gravestone for both her parents was erected in the town cemetery in a far more opulent style than would be expected for cloth mill workers, and Dorcas's new life may well have been the catalyst for that.

As the century wore on, the Clark woollen mills operation was consolidated on the Studley Mills site from 1884, and the Duke Street Mills and Stone Mills were sold on. Trowbridge continued to boom as a centre for cloth manufacture, and the fortunes of Dorcas and Thomas with it. He was known around the area as Major Tom rather than Thomas. As he grew older, he is mentioned more in political circles in the area, being one of a cluster of staunch Conservative businessmen, and Dorcas occasionally gets a newspaper mention at having been at political gatherings at his side. He does not seem to have entertained ideas of standing as a candidate, however, unlike his peers.

As could perhaps be expected given their difference in ages, Major Tom died while Dorcas was still relatively young, at the age of 79, in September 1899. She then seems to have withdrawn from visible public life, for the most part. She was involved in a memorial window for her husband at St Thomas's church, the one he had had built in 1870, which was unveiled in 1903.

The cloth industry in Trowbridge began to decline during the early 20th century, with stiff competition from mills in Yorkshire, and many of the Trowbridge woollen mill buildings took on a different purpose. Bridge Mills became a corn mill. Cradle Bridge Mills made mattresses. Castle Court Mills became a brush manufacturer. Yerbury Street Mills produced rubber. Clarks kept going, having consolidated their business, and Dorcas's personal finances must have been tied to that firm and their investments, alongside any inheritance that Thomas had left her.

However, in 1903 some pieces of the Clark estate land were sold off, including Great Cumberwell, at South Wraxall, which may have been Dorcas consolidating finances or deciding that she no longer wished to run the affairs of that estate.

Many women of her class and station became more involved in public life as the 20th century went on, with widows, wives and daughters of the bigger houses encouraged to join voluntary aid detachments from 1909, and become involved in housing Belgian refugees from the early days of the First World War. However, there is no mention of Dorcas in any of these capacities. She seems to have lived quietly at Bellefield, with loyal servant Amy Sheppard – employed by her as cook and general servant from at least 1901, and gave her occupation on censuses as of private means, so therefore living on inheritance and investments. She was known to have absolutely adored the deer in her private deer park at Bellefield, and been involved in the life and worship of St Thomas's Church.

Dorcas passed away in January 1938, aged 90, and the *Wiltshire Times and Trowbridge Advertiser* mourned one of the last links with the Trowbridge of Victorian days. Her funeral was held in St Thomas's church, and there were many mourners from the Clark family and their descendants. There is no mention in the list of attendees of any relatives from her Pearce or Pierce family, though the paper does mention her previous surname and the fact that she had been a previous Clark Mills employee. It appears that her more humble background and the unusual nature of her marriage was easier to report upon in the more relaxed society in the run up to the Second World War than it was in the tightly class-regimented 1870s, but the feelings of Dorcas's birth relatives about the marriage and her elevation to high society are not recorded anywhere.

Bellefield was sold off, to a Mr William Thomas of Maidenhead, but the 14 deer in the park did not go with the house, as Dorcas's will had stipulated that they were to be given to someone who would not kill them. After various wranglings, they were eventually captured and sent off to a new life in Scotland.

Mr Thomas didn't take up residence in Bellefield, however, and the house was requisitioned for American soldiers in the run up to D-Day in the Second World War. Afterwards, the Ministry of National Insurance had the house, while the surrounding land had houses built upon it. Later on, it became the headquarters for Unigate and St Ivel dairies, and today houses Zircon Software, a computer company.

References

Bath Chronicle and Weekly Gazette, 14 September 1899, Funeral of Major Clark
Bath Chronicle and Weekly Gazette, 2 April 1938 Trowbridge Deer
Clifton Society, 21 January 1904, Bath
Daily News (London), 11 March 1938, Herd of Deer No-one Wants
Devizes and Wiltshire Gazette, 31 March 1859, Trowbridge – the late Thomas Clark
Devizes and Wiltshire Gazette, 20 November 1890, Gross Slander on Major Clark, of Trowbridge
Devizes and Wiltshire Gazette, 9 November 1905, Presentation to the Reverend N Thwaites
Edinburgh Evening News, 14 March 1938, English Deer Herd for Scotland
England and Wales 1921 census, held by Findmypast.co.uk
England & Wales, National Probate Calendar (Index of Wills and Administrations), 1858-1995
England & Wales, Civil Registration Birth Index, 1837-1915, held by Ancestry.co.uk
England & Wales, Civil Registration Death Index, 1916-2007 held by Ancestry.co.uk
England & Wales, Civil Registration Marriage Index, 1837-1915 held by Ancestry.co.uk
Marlborough Times, 23 September 1882, Wanted
Marlborough Times, 14 May 1887, Wanted
Marlborough Times, 8 October 1892, Wanted
Northamptonshire, England, Church of England Marriages, 1754-1912, held by Ancestry.co.uk
Northampton Mercury, 11 October 1873, Stanwick
Pall Mall Gazette, 12 October 1876, Marriages
Salisbury and Winchester Journal, 26 February 1870, Trowbridge
Somerset Standard, 15 September 1899, Trowbridge – Death of Major Clark
Trowbridge Chronicle, 21 October 1876, Marriage of Major Clark
Trowbridge Chronicle, 21 November 1891, Death and Burial of Mrs Henry Clark

UK Census Collection, held by Ancestry.co.uk
Victoria County History (1953), *A History of the County of Wiltshire*: Volume 7, London
Western Daily Press, 13 October 1876, Marriages
Wiltshire, England, Church of England Births and Baptisms, 1813-1922, held by Ancestry.co.uk
Wiltshire, England, Church of England Deaths and Burials, 1813-1922, held by Ancestry.co.uk
Wiltshire, England, Church of England Marriages and Banns, 1754-1916, held by Ancestry.co.uk
Wiltshire County Mirror, 31 October 1893, Parlourmaid or House-parlourmaid
Wiltshire Times and Trowbridge Advertiser, 11 November 1876, Return of Major and Mrs Clark
Wiltshire Times and Trowbridge Advertiser, 9 September 1899, Death of Major T Clark, J.P.
Wiltshire Times and Trowbridge Advertiser, 22 January 1938, Death of Mrs Dorcas Clark
Wiltshire Times and Trowbridge Advertiser, 29 January 1938, Re Dorcas Clark deceased
Wiltshire Times and Trowbridge Advertiser, 29 January 1938, Bellefield Memories
Wiltshire Times and Trowbridge Advertiser, 26 February 1938 When politics were politics
Wiltshire Times and Trowbridge Advertiser, 12 March 1938, Foley, Son and Mundy
Wiltshire Times and Trowbridge Advertiser, 7 May 1938 The Dodging Deer
Wiltshire Times and Trowbridge Advertiser, 23 July 1938, The Bellefield Estate
Wiltshire Times and Trowbridge Advertiser, 8 March 1947, Bellefield House

Amy Aylward

MUSIC RAN IN Amy Aylward's blood, body and soul. So much so that her musician father actually named her after his favourite piano manufacturer – Metzler. Metzler and Co. made pianos in London from 1833 until 1931, and her father would have been very familiar with their instruments.

The youngest of eight, and the fourth daughter, Amy Metzler Aylward experienced an extremely musical childhood in Salisbury. Born at the beginning of 1852, at the time her father William Aylward was making a very decent living teaching piano and selling music, excelling at playing the flute and operating as a church organist (although not at Salisbury cathedral) and was a military bandsman. He also conducted the Sarum Choral Society. Her mother was Sarah, née Conduit, and Amy's siblings were William, Albert, Janetta, Leila, Theodore, Augustus, and Gertrude. All of Amy's siblings took up music, and are referred to as ‹professor of music› on documents from an early age, indicating that talent was rife within the family.

Round about the time she was born, her sister Janetta was elected King's Scholar of the Royal Academy of Music. Janetta's instrument wasn't made clear in the reports of her achievement, but it is likely to have been either voice or piano, or at a push violin – as these instruments were considered the most suitable for women at that time. Very occasionally, a woman is noted as a 'cellist. Other orchestral instruments were the preserve of men. Her eldest brother William – a 'cellist of some renown – was also given the same King's Scholar position two years earlier in 1850.

While William went on to excel, playing in orchestras and taking prestigious positions – for example, with the Orchestra of the Royal Italian Opera, and later teaching music at Eton, Janetta reportedly worked too hard, became ill and died in London at the age of 15 and a half.

Much of Amy's family life would have revolved around her father's music room business. They bought, sold and repaired musical instruments in their large saloon in the centre of the city. This was also a venue for concerts of all sorts. The building has long since been demolished and replaced. The family had lived in The Close in the city, close to the cathedral, but also above their music emporium at New Canal.

Her father's business promoted concerts at the Assembly Rooms in Salisbury, today bookshop Waterstones on the High Street, on one occasion in 1872 both advertising a concert with full orchestra on April 17, and an exhibition performance on April 2 by pianist Charles Hallé (founder of the Hallé Orchestra) and violinist Madam Wilma Norman-Neruda. This couple married a few years later.

Adverts for the business, later William Price Aylward in partnership with his son Augustus, and by 1887 known as Aylward and Spinney, offered pianofortes, American organs, and harmoniums. They also offered a selection of stringed instruments, and repairs, and a huge selection of sheet music. They employed a piano and organ tuner, and had a full music library for people to browse.

Against this background, and with a huge amount of innate talent, Amy's musicality would have been encouraged and fostered.

Later on in Amy's childhood, her brother Augustus – a celebrated double bassist – became the organist at Salisbury's St Thomas Church, while her brother Theodore took up a similar position at first Chichester Cathedral and then Llandaff Cathedral, near Cardiff.

Amy herself specialised in singing, like her older sister Leila. Amy possessed a high soprano voice, which became a distinguishing feature. And she also played the piano.

The family were well to do, with servants in the household, and her father employed an organ tuner on his staff. This comfortable background enabled Amy and her siblings to have the space and time to excel in their musical talent, as they did not have to work to survive. Her father served as an Alderman, and later was mayor for Salisbury in 1869.

Following the path of her next oldest sister Gertrude, Amy travelled to Germany in early adulthood to study opera singing at the Stuttgart Conservatoire. Today the Conservatoire is the Staatliche Hochschule für Musik und Darstellende Kunst Stuttgart, or the State University of Music and Performing Arts Stuttgart. This school was founded in 1857, as the Stuttgart Music School, but became the musical conservatoire for the Kingdom of Wurttemberg in 1869. The school was well-renowned for its piano teaching at that time, so would have been an obvious choice for Amy's musical training, with celebrated teachers being Sigismund Lebert and Mr Prüchner. Lebert, in partnership with Ludwig Stark, was a technical specialist, and popularised a particular style of piano practice where fingers were tightly regulated.

While it may have been unusual for an upper-middle-class young woman to be sent so far away for training, the musical lifestyle then – as it does today – required a huge amount of travel for engagements and concerts. The Aylward family were seasoned travellers.

By 1876, Amy was back in London, studying at the Royal Academy of Music under celebrated conductor Alberto Randegger. Italian-born Randegger was a specialist in vocal music, and had been professor of singing at the Royal Academy from 1857 onwards. Amy, having earlier trained hard on the piano, was intent on improving her other musical skills.

The Academy at the time was an amalgamation of three 18th century houses in Tenterden Street, Hanover Square in London.

As a result of this specialist training, the local papers made much of her success. The *Hampshire Advertiser*, on 6 September 1876, said:

> The many friends and admirers in this city of Miss Amy Aylward, of Salisbury (niece of our esteemed townsman Mr. A. Conduit) will be rejoiced to hear of her continued success at the Royal Academy of Music, and her recent taking of prizes at the annual competitive concert of the

Academy, held at St. James's Hall last week, where, for her execution of C. Novello's 'Thy Mighty Power,' she was awarded the bronze medal of the R.A.M. She was also commended for the part she took in the Parepa Rosa Gold Medal competition; and she was awarded a prize for her proficiency in 'second studies'. Madame Christine Nillson present the rewards. Miss Aylward's well-trained and melodious soprano has been frequently heard and enjoyed by large audiences in the city.

Her sister Gertrude would often be her accompanist and duet partner. Amy had a performing career, often appearing in public. The training she received at specialist institutions had notable enhanced her voice. The *Hampshire Advertiser* in April 1878 said:

> Miss Amy Aylward of Salisbury was the chief solo singer, and she was, we think, never in better voice, her expression, her pure utterance, and her execution being greatly admired.

Although chiefly based in Salisbury, she also performed elsewhere – Bristol, Ryde on the Isle of Wight, Weymouth, Plymouth, Sheffield, The *Weymouth Telegram*, in 1878, said:

> Miss Amy Aylward of the Crystal Palace Concerts and Royal Academy of Music proved a great attraction, and on every appearance was received with applause.

A review of a concert in Bristol's Colston Hall in 1879 said that Amy's singing was promising, adding that: 'Her register is a considerable range, and besides excelling in brilliant passages she displays sympathetic expression.'

By the early 1880s, Amy was regularly giving a series of her own concerts in Salisbury, trading on her well-known name and expertise. These were also well received in the local area. She booked other musicians, but also performed herself alongside them, much as her father had been doing for decades.

> Miss Aylward gave her last concert of the season in the Assembly Rooms, on the afternoon of Tuesday, the audience being by far the largest of any previous occasion. The programme was of that high class character which has marked the series of musical entertainments given by her, and

it is satisfactory to note how thoroughly the whole of them have been appreciated,

said the *Hampshire Advertiser* in December 1882.

Amy's mother Sarah died in 1879 in Salisbury. Her father married for a second time to widow Mary Marie Harriet Synnot (née Preston) in 1884. She was known to all as Maimie.

A report of a concert given by St Martin's Choral Society in *Salisbury Times* in April 1885, said:

Miss Aylward sang with taste, with graceful verve, and in pleasant voice, her characteristic tremulo occasionally (as in the intermediate solo in 'With a laugh as we go round') making her music all the prettier. The duet 'Can I not find,' which she sang with Mr Howgate, was a charming bit of harmony.

These concerts appear to have been a regular occurrence during the first half of the 1880s, and she is known to have often performed at the Musical Society in Cambridge, and the Monday Popular Concerts. However, she suffered periods of ill-health which forced her to retire from the stage. Instead, she made her living by teaching.

Her father died in Salisbury in September 1890, and was widely mourned. This seems to have released Amy from family responsibilities, and instead she took her career to the capital.

By the early 1890s she was well established as a singing teacher and a professor of music in London, living alongside another unmarried sister – Leila – who also described herself as a professor of music on the 1891 census return.

Amy seems to have primarily taught in London, but made weekly visits to towns in Essex to take pupils at Milton Mount College. Adverts for her teaching in Gravesend begin in 1893 and continue through until at least 1903. She was teaching vocalisation in English, French, German and Italian – primarily operatic languages, which were perhaps the influence of her teacher Randeggar at the Royal Academy, as he was a known expert in opera.

Later on, Leila moved back to Salisbury to continue teaching and accompanying the local choral society, so Amy went to live with her next oldest sister Gertrude. This sister, it was claimed, was the most musically talented of them all – but had had to retire from the profession when she married a doctor, as women of her station in life did not make their own living, however prodigiously talented they were. It's likely that Gertrude still played, but in private and among family. Amy herself never married, so was able to keep her talent and teaching career. It is unknown if she ever had any serious relationship.

Amy and Gertrude lived together from the 1890s onwards in London. Initially this was on Albany Street, near Regent's Park, and Amy taught out of her sister's home while her doctor brother-in-law continued to practice. They then moved to St Andrew's Place, where Amy's brother-in-law – Charles Chinner Fuller – died in 1902. By 1911 Amy and Gertrude were together at an address in Hampstead, close to Primrose Hill. They had several servants, and a South African boarder – a vocalist who was presumably a pupil or associate of Amy's – living with them.

By 1921 Amy was still teaching singing in London, but also doing part-time secretarial work alongside her sister Gertrude – who, as the propriety of restrictions on women working was easing, was working for the Medical Society of London.

Amy lived until 1923, leaving her assets to her sister Gertrude. Her namesake niece, the daughter of her brother Augustus, had her own singing and teaching career but in the changing times was able to continue performing even after her own marriage.

References

Bell's Weekly Messenger, 20 June 1853 Miss Janetta Aylward
Carl Rosa Trust (2016) The Rosa Troupe, Alberto Randegger, at https://www.carlrosatrust.org.uk/troupe/troupe_Randegger.html (accessed 28.9.2024)
Devizes and Wiltshire Gazette, 30 December 1852 We see from the London papers that...
England and Wales 1921 census, held by Findmypast.co.uk
England & Wales, Civil Registration Birth Index, 1837-1915, held by Ancestry.co.uk
England & Wales, Civil Registration Marriage Index, 1837-1915, held by Ancestry.co.uk
England & Wales, Civil Registration Death Index, 1835-1915, held by Ancestry.co.uk
England & Wales, National Probate Calendar (Index of Wills and Administrations), 1858-1995, held by Ancestry.co.uk
Gravesend & Northfleet Standard, 30 September 1893 Miss Amy Aylward

Gravesend Reporter, North Kent and South Essex Advertiser, 16 February 1901 Miss Amy Aylward
Gravesend Reporter, North Kent and South Essex Advertiser, 21 February 1903 Miss Amy Aylward
Hampshire Advertiser, 25 December 1852 Musical honours
Hampshire Advertiser, 6 September 1876, Music success
Hampshire Advertiser, 2 December 1882 Miss Aylward's Concert
Hampshire Chronicle, 20 September 1890 The funeral of the late Alderman Aylward
Hants and Berks Gazette and Middlesex and Surrey Journal, 24 October 1903 The Aylward Family
Isle of Wight Journal, 8 September 1877 New Town Hall, Ryde
Horniman Museum and Gardens, Metzler & Co. at https://www.horniman.ac.uk/agent/agent-5936/ (accessed 28/9/2024)
Limerick Chronicle, 15 June 1853 Deaths
Musical World (1869), W H Aylward Vol. 47, Iss. 15
Musical Times and Singing Class Circular (1.1.1853) Brief Chronicle of the Last Month Vol. 5, No. 104, pp. 124-126 (3 pages)
Practicing the piano (2024) Don't Try This at Home! – Mechanical Aids to Practice https://practisingthepiano.com/dont-try-home/
Salisbury and Winchester Journal, 11 June 1853 Deaths
Salisbury and Winchester Journal, 22 January 1887 Aylward and Spinney
Salisbury and Winchester Journal, 30 March 1872 Assembly Rooms Salisbury
Salisbury Times, 25 April 1885 St Martin's Choral Society
Salisbury Times, 17 January 1891 William Price Aylward deceased
Sheffield Daily Telegraph, 26 October 1877 Madame Arabella Goddard
Staatliche Hochschule für Musik und Darstellende Kunst Stuttgart (2024), History of the University, at https://www.hmdk-stuttgart.de/about/history-of-the-university/?L=1&fbclid=IwAR1dsNFRB68M8PZhzQ3lti6YdUxzz81MrfRgz_qJOfmD1XYp8uONhV1T_hg (accessed 28.9.2024)
UK Census collection, held by Ancestry.co.uk
Western Daily Press, 18 November 1879 Popular Concert at Colston Hall
Western Morning News, 7 December 1877, Arabella Goddard
Weymouth Telegram, 30 August 1878, Amateur Concert
Wiltshire, England, Church of England Births and Baptisms, 1813-1922, held by Ancestry.co.uk
Wiltshire, England, Church of England Marriages and Banns, 1754-1916, held by Ancestry.co.uk
Wiltshire, England, Church of England Deaths and Burials, 1813-1922 held by Ancestry.co.uk
Wiltshire, England, Marriages, 1538-1837, held by Ancestry.co.uk

Freelove Priscilla Noad or Wastfield or Sims

THE RATHER 1960S-SOUNDING Freelove was actually born in the early 1820s, about 140 years too early for the hippy nature of her name, but seems to have led an unconventional life nonetheless. Named after her paternal grandmother, she married twice (including to her sort-of cousin), ran a pub in Bradford-on-Avon despite being religiously opposed to alcohol, was subject to divorce proceedings in the 1870s, and finally suffered a mental health breakdown so badly that she was placed in the local asylum.

Despite invoking a vision of promiscuity, psychedelic guitars and patchouli oil, Freelove as a name is distinctly Anglo-Saxon and Old English in origin, and – though slightly more common as a surname rather than first name – seems beloved of non-conformist families in the later 1700s and into the 1800s. This fits with her family background, as they appear to have been of the Baptist faith, based around Rowde, Devizes and Littleton Wood – though Freelove herself was based in Bradford-on-Avon and further south into Wiltshire.

Her father, William Noad, was a millwright in Littleton Wood, a tiny place of a few dwellings near the village of Semington. His background seems to have been relatively well-off in a rural setting, but the family's historical background was pre-industrial, so he would have built on increasing mill technology at that time rather than being an industrialist.

Freelove's mother was Ann, but – on account of the scarcity of non-conformist records – her maternal family background has been lost as her parents' marriage hasn't come to light. Freelove had at least an older sister, Elizabeth, and brother, Simon. She was born around 1822 at Bowerhill, close to Melksham, but also sometimes seems to have given her birthdate as around 1826, so it is possible that she wasn't actually her purported father's child. He had drowned in 1823, in a pond on his property at Littleton Wood, aged 41 (not long after another un-named sibling of Freelove had died aged 15 weeks) and was buried alongside his mother at Devizes Baptist church. Either Freelove had been born before his demise, or her mother was pregnant at his death, or she wasn't actually his child. Either way, she would have grown up without a father.

The Littleton Wood property went to her uncle Stephen Noad, and her mother was left money in his will, but does not seem to have been able to make it last, as by the time the 1841 census was taken both Freelove and Elizabeth were working as domestic servants in Bradford-on-Avon, and their brother Simon was a stable keeper and groom in Bath. Their family background would seem to have precluded the possibility that Simon could have also been an educated business owner rather than working with horses, and that Freelove and Elizabeth should not have been working – so the economic condition of their family had clearly deteriorated after William Noad's death.

Freelove's saving grace appears to have been her father's older sister Ann Noad, who had married Job Wastfield in 1819 and was also living in Bradford-on-Avon at the same time as her nieces were working there. The Wastfield family were local entrepreneurs and engineers, working in the cloth and wool trade in Bradford-on-Avon as the textile business was really starting to boom at that town. Job Wastfield, alongside his brother John, had the patent of a sheep-shearing frame from 1812 onwards, which made the process more efficient. He also, more importantly, owned a cloth mill.

In his later years, Job was also the licensee of The Plough Inn, on Trowbridge Road in Bradford-on-Avon – although it was more likely that his wife Ann ran the pub while he was working on other business. They took in their nephew, another Job Wastfield, son of his brother William, who was to become Freelove's first husband. Though also involved in cloth milling, he also brewed the beer for the establishment, and at some point after 1841 the pub took in Ann's niece Freelove who had been employed as a servant round the corner in the bigger houses at Regent's Place.

Job Wastfield the elder died in 1847, leaving his properties and his pub to his wife Ann, and by the time of the 1851 census the three of them – Ann, Job-the-younger and Freelove were running the pub together. Ann was the innkeeper, Job the brewer, and Freelove the barmaid. Though Job and Freelove were Ann's nephew and niece respectively, they weren't actually cousins to each other.

It is possible that Ann regarded them as such though, as they didn't actually marry each other until Ann had died in 1852. Ann passed away in the spring of 1852, and Freelove and Job married that October. This also meant that Freelove had a promotion, from barmaid to landlady, and she may well have been completely in charge of the premises, leaving Job to his other interests, even though – as a married woman – her husband had to hold the licence to sell alcohol.

The Plough likely did very well on account of passing trade. The inn was - and still is - on the main road from Bradford-on-Avon to Trowbridge. It would have been a regular stop for market traders along the road, as well as any other people passing between the two towns, and probably saw steady trade from carriers and hauliers along the road too. There was also an iron foundry nearby, whose workers would have frequented it, and a fair amount of people in the community would have regarded it as their local too. This would have meant that Freelove's finances were on the up.

She and Job had a son, named Job after his father and great uncle, in 1853, but no more children came along. However, her husband Job was not in the best of health, and – anticipating the end – began making a will in 1855. Freelove was to have the pub, and several family-owned properties on Bradford-on-Avon's St Margaret's Hill, and he also made provision for Freelove's sister Elizabeth too. Job died in 1857, of Bright's Disease – a loss of kidney function that today is called nephritis - when he was 43. Their son Job would have been around four years old. Freelove erected a gravestone in his memory.

Accordingly, Freelove took on the licence of The Plough, becoming landlady in actuality rather than name. Single women – if they were unmarried, divorced or widowed – were allowed to hold the licence of a pub at this time, and many did. But as soon as she was married, her husband had to go to the local magistrates and have the licence switched to him instead, even if he had no intention of running the pub day-to-day. She held the position as landlady for several years, bringing up her son in the building and employing her sister Elizabeth to help her out. She also seems to have spent some time with Job's sister Elizabeth, who was based in Wyke Regis near Weymouth in Dorset, as she had her son Job baptised into the Church of England in that area in 1861, moving gradually away from the Baptist faith. Round about the same time, she suffered the first bout of mental illness which was to come to define her later life, but received no formal treatment or diagnosis, and was considered recovered in the eyes of her community and society.

Freelove's second marriage, though looking ideal on paper, was perhaps not the greatest choice of new partner, in hindsight.

James Sims, the local butcher, who was based in Bradford-on-Avon's old marketplace, seems to have been a solid local citizen, and involved in various local organisations and institutions. He was a widower, having lost his first wife Ann in 1864, and had a daughter – Emma – about the same age as Freelove's son Job. The union between them, in 1867, was at a respectful distance from the passing of their former partners, and two successful business owners marrying must have seemed to be a good match. He taught Freelove's son Job the butchering trade too, setting him up for life.

Freelove gave up the licence of The Plough – James could have taken on the licence had he wished, and she could have continued to run it, but that clearly wasn't the plan. The Mizen family took over the pub, and Freelove went to live with James at his business premises. She, given her experience of working with the public, probably worked alongside him in the butcher's shop. The premises of that shop moved about the town somewhat, but it was always relatively central. It may be that the loss of her autonomy may have sat uneasily with Freelove from the beginning, but the cracks in the marriage started to show in the summer of 1876, about nine years in when she was around the age of 47.

The first glimmer that something wasn't right is written in two local newspapers on 1 July 1876, when it appeared that Freelove had been publicly extremely drunk, and had caused a ruckus outside her husband's shop on the 29 May that year. She'd been beating the shutters and calling for her husband, so it sounds like they were not in the best of places in their relationship.

The police tried to intervene, telling her to pack it in and to go home, but she refused so was taken home by police escort. When she appeared in front of the magistrates, around a month later, she was charged with drunk and disorderly conduct. She firstly denied she'd done it in the first place, and secondly – when it was clear she wasn't being believed – she apparently offered no proper defence of her actions. She was fined 10 shillings and a further eight shillings for the costs of bringing her case to court, and instructed by the court not to do it again. There is no further report of her in any newspaper.

Public drunkenness, particularly on the part of a woman, was very frowned upon by society at this time. Women certainly drank, and in Freelove's case – as a former pub landlady – she probably had more leeway than most, but it was usually in private settings and in moderation. Public drunkenness was seen as the realm of the very lowest in society, who in the perception of the time would have been far from good, godly and upright behaviour. Her actions may have threatened her husband James's good standing in the town, and it certainly would have harmed her reputation.

However, husband James was not finished yet. Within a month, he had filed for divorce from Freelove.

Divorce at this time was rare, but not unheard of. It is often perceived as the preserve of the very rich, since cases had to be heard at the High Court in London and this required accommodation in that city while proceedings progressed on top of the legal fees – but it was not out of the realms of affordability for a successful business owner with few dependants. James decided that the expense was worth a shot at getting out of a marriage that wasn't working, and went for it.

The case, filed on 20 July 1876, accused Freelove of adultery with Charles Long – who appears to have possibly been either a married quarry owner or his son, or possibly a carpenter – which took place at their Whitehill Lane residence on the night before her drunken attack on James's shop. So, the accusation was almost certainly part of the row.

Both Charles and Freelove denied the allegations. Charles was approached by the court on 9 August 1876, and said there was no truth in them. Freelove was interviewed a day later, and also said that she had not committed adultery with Charles. It may have been that Charles was a friend who had kindly offered Freelove lodging space after her row with James, and James had jumped to conclusions. But despite these denials, James still sought the end of his marriage and persisted with the case.

Proceedings were heard in London on the 25 and 27 of April 1877. However, the judge found in favour of Freelove and Charles, and dismissed the case, so the marriage remained. James was also ordered to pay his own costs, as well as the legal fees for Charles and Freelove.

Two months later, however, circumstances changed which meant that James could not have another stab at ending their marriage. Freelove suffered a second bout of mental illness and was admitted to a private lunatic asylum near Salisbury.

Fisherton House Asylum, later the Old Manor Hospital, was founded as a private facility in the early 19th century, and seems to have been on a different scale than the county lunatic asylum for Wiltshire, which was at Roundway, near Devizes. Alongside specialising in the treatment of criminal lunatics before the establishment of Broadmoor, the facility took paupers and paying patients, from across the south west, but it is unclear from Freelove's case notes on which basis she was there. There may have been enough income from her inherited properties from first husband Job to pay for her care.

Her case notes say that she was 48 years old, and of the Wesleyan faith, so one of the branches of Methodism. This should mean that she habitually didn't drink, as Methodists eschewed alcohol – but were usually fine with selling it to those who did – which puts her public drunkenness of the previous year in a different light. She was regarded as the wife of a butcher from Bradford-on-Avon, and had grey-ish hair and light brown eyes. The certificate of insanity from her initial assessment says:

> Inability to hold a rational conversation, simply asserts that she cannot lie down, cannot rest, cannot eat because there is no time. She is in a state of the utmost dejection and melancholy.

The combination these symptoms, with her age and the rather public ending of her marriage, points to the idea that she was perhaps going through the hormonal changes associated with peri-menopause, and this had dipped into depression and exacerbated her earlier issues. Fisherton Asylum would have treated the symptoms, but would not have had the medical knowledge of the following 160 years to address the underlying causes. She was considered not epileptic, not dangerous, and did not seem to have issues with alcohol.

Freelove is recorded as having issues with eating, refusing to do so and wandering about in an absent manner when attempts were made to make her eat. To treat this, the hospital decided to tube feed her once a day. This would be the type of unsophisticated tube feeding that is more commonly associated with force-fed imprisoned and hunger-striking suffragettes during the early 20th century, but was in existence long before. The patient was held down, a tube inserted up the nasal passage, and food poured down into the body via a funnel and jug. It was unsophisticated, invasive, and painful.

So much so that by 3 August 1877, Freelove's case notes report that she had a great horror of the tube, and willingly ate breakfast and dinner that day. However, things did not improve and she was still being force fed by tube until that November.

However, while her issues around food improved, her general mental health did not. Her case notes into 1880 report that she would often secrete herself somewhere in the grounds of the hospital, and stare vacantly for hours upon end. Despite being literate enough to write her own name on both her wedding certificates, the hospital considered her 'of very feeble intelligence but of good bodily health'.

Freelove remained at Fisherton, without ever leaving and probably not seeing her son either, until her death there in the October of 1894, when she was 68 years old. She was buried alongside her first husband Job in Bradford-on-Avon.

Not letting the grass grow under his feet, her erstwhile husband James – who had not been able to end the marriage by any other means – remarried the following February to a woman thirty years his junior.

Freelove's son Job initially worked as a butcher in Tisbury, and then at Wardour, both near Salisbury. One of his children was given the middle name Freelove after his mother.

References

Devizes and Wiltshire Gazette, 2 August 1827, Bulkington Mill
England, Select Dorset Church of England Parish Registers, 1538-1999, held by Ancestry.co.uk
England & Wales, Births, Marriages and Deaths indexes, 1837-1915, held by Ancestry.co.uk
England & Wales, Civil Divorce Records, 1858-1918, held by Ancestry.co.uk

England & Wales, Non-Conformist and Non-Parochial Registers, 1567-1936, held by Ancestry.co.uk

England & Wales, Prerogative Court of Canterbury Wills, 1384-1858, held by Ancestry.co.uk

Kelly's Directory of Wiltshire, 1898

Patient Case Books of Fisherton Anger Lunatic Asylum, held by Wiltshire and Swindon History Centre

Post Office Directory of Hampshire, Wiltshire & Dorsetshire, 1855

Post Office Directory of Wiltshire, 1859

Probate records of the Archdeaconry of Salisbury 1824, held by Ancestry.co.uk

Probate records of the Archdeaconry of Salisbury 1857, held by Ancestry.co.uk

Robson's Directory of the Western Counties (Member LE Compendium), 1839

Salisbury and Winchester Journal, 31 August 1812, Daniell's Patent Shearing Frames

Trowbridge and North Wiltshire Advertiser, 1 July 1876, Bradford on Avon Petty Sessions: Drunkenness

Trowbridge Chronicle, 1 July 1876, Another drunk and disorderly

UK, Lunacy Patients Admission Registers, 1846-1921, held by Ancestry.co.uk

UK Census collection, held by Ancestry.co.uk

Wiltshire, England, Church of England Baptisms, Marriages and Burials, 1538-1812, held by Ancestry.co.uk

Wiltshire, England, Church of England Marriages and Banns, 1754-1916, held by Ancestry.co.uk

Wiltshire Independent, 1 July 1852, Deaths

Wiltshire Independent, 21 October 1852, Marriages

Wiltshire Times and Trowbridge Advertiser, 3 June 1865, Bradford on Avon Ancient Order of Foresters

Susannah Smith

WHAT TO DO with a large pot of money when you didn't have any dependants or descendants was a dilemma for elderly or ill unmarried Victorian women of means? Often nieces and nephews came into the inheritance, but if they were already married or successful, or didn't exist in the first place, something had to be done with the funds past the cost of your funeral.

The top choice for many in that position was to donate it to good and deserving causes, so that the less fortunate could benefit. Some women would set up a charity to be administered through their church. Others – like Elizabeth Utterson in Chippenham – built and funded almshouses for good and godly souls who had fallen on harder times. Some would give to established charities. Some would fund building projects that would directly benefit the local population – for example, a facility at a workhouse, or a new hospital wing, or even cutting-edge health technology for that hospital.

Susannah Smith of Warminster fell into the latter category, as her donated money funded a new wing of the town's cottage hospital. Eliza Vicary, who at one point lived next door to Susannah, also donated funds to build another wing of the same hospital.

Susannah was born in Bath in 1810, but arrived in Warminster – where her father had been born – in the mid-19th century to care for a recently widowed uncle, and clearly loved the town and its people dearly.

She was baptised in St James, Bath, in June 1810, the daughter of Gaius Smith and Sarah née Millard. She was their second child, and the only girl with four brothers. Her father Gaius seems to have been relatively well to do – he was an upholsterer, chairmaker and cabinet maker serving the middle and upper classes of Bath. This, though a manual profession, took training and honing of skills, and was far from a hand-to-mouth existence.

However, other than her younger brothers' baptism records which place the family at Bradley's Buildings in Southgate Street during the second decade of the 19th century, there is very little evidence of Susannah actually in Bath. Because she didn't marry, and census records didn't include names until 1841, there is no physical record of her in the town past her baptism. Her father died in 1830, when she was around 19, and an executrix – presumably her mother – sold his business accoutrements from the house on Southgate Street.

While her mother and younger brothers were at home at 28 Southgate Street in Bath, once named census records begin, and her eldest brother Bennet was working as a butcher in Wellow in Somerset, Susannah had already relocated to Warminster. She lived with her mother's sister Martha, and her husband John Case, on the town's Portway. She may have been with them since childhood, as Martha and John didn't have any children of their own – and in those cases a niece or nephew might become a child of the household. John Case was a proprietor of houses, which meant someone who rented houses out to people rather than an estate agent. Susannah was given as an independent annuitant, so someone who had her own financial independence. She had probably inherited money from her father.

While her younger brother Gaius became a book binder and seller, and her brother Seth was an upholsterer like her father, the family's condition meant that Susannah did not need to work. She may have had an unacknowledged role within her uncle's business, and after her aunt's death in 1855 she seems to have been more involved, as she was given as a proprietor as well as a fundholder with her uncle on the 1861 census. That year also saw the death of her mother, and her uncle. Her brother Bennett, who had been living in Dunkerton, south of Bath, committed suicide that year too.

The Warminster Cottage Hospital, which was to become Susannah's passion, was founded round the corner from her home on Portway in 1866. That year the Marquess of Bath gave a small farm and garden for the purpose, which was enough space to provide a doctor and two nurses to improve access to medical care for people unable to travel to bigger settlements. These few beds would have improved the general health of the town, which was a driving force for good works in the Victorian era and saw many similar facilities set up across British towns.

Susannah was the main inheritor and executrix of her uncle's will, and probably kept up the renting of his properties. She moved from Portway to East Street by 1871, where she took in a lodger – the property was probably too big for one person, and this would have increased the amount of money she was able to give to her passion projects – and had a servant, Emily Cox. Emily's four-year-old illegitimate daughter Kate was also in the household. Susannah later lived at 6 Boreham Villas, which were smaller and more humble properties than her money could have afforded her.

Emily seems to have stayed in Susannah's service for a long time. She married a soldier, William Cowdry, from Susannah's house in 1879. Her daughter Kate stayed with Susannah however, and she also took in a niece, Anna, who had been born in Bath, which paints Susannah as a particularly kind person. The household was still set at Boreham Terrace in 1881.

Through the cottage hospital, and other good works Susannah probably knew fellow hospital supporter Eliza Hester Vicary. Scottish-born Eliza had come to Warminster after her father had died in Ilfracombe, Devon. She appears to have been a relative of George Vicary, who was the local doctor, but not a close one as she did not live with the main family and instead made her home at Boreham Villas. An only child, again in possession of quite a bit of money with no dependants, Eliza was very much respected in the town, and when she died in 1888 she left money to build a new wing of the hospital. The *Warminster and Westbury Journal* said at the time of her death:

> Although possessed of a highly cultivated mind and of many accomplishments, Miss Vicary was chiefly remarkable for the two great virtues of humility and charity. Her friends will long remember her as one who ever sought to avoid hurting the feelings of others, who never was heard to speak an uncharitable word, and who always used her stores of

knowledge for the improvement and instruction of those amongst whom she lived. The poor had in her a real friend: her many acts of judicious charity were performed in strict accordance with the gospel precept; no one knew the good she did; but the cessation of her loving ministry to the sick and needy will be widely felt, her relief and needy will be widely felt, her relief and counsel sorely missed, and her death sincerely mourned.'

Susannah seems to have been of the same mindset as Eliza, and the pair probably worked together in support of the hospital. Eliza left £300 to the hospital to enable a new wing to be built, but this was not completed until 1892, when a further donation – from the bequest of Maria Baily Vicary, daughter of doctor George Vicary and some sort of cousin to Eliza – was added to the pot. The new wing, called the Vicary Wing, had a women's convalescent ward, a probationers' room and a laboratory, and then a women's ward upstairs, opened in April 1892 with a religious ceremony and tea party on the lawn. Susannah was probably in attendance.

Susannah's benevolence towards the hospital continued. In September 1897, less than two years after the technology was invented, she presented the doctors with an X-ray machine. This was at this stage called a 'Roentgen Ray apparatus', after its inventor. Wilhelm Conrad Röntgen, a German scientist, had been working with radiation. In November 1895 he had realised the medical use of his work when he'd made a picture of his wife's hand using X-radiation, and immediately began writing to medical journals with his discovery. By the time Susannah purchased the apparatus for the Warminster hospital, the technology was still cutting edge but starting to be rolled out across the medical profession, and would have had vast implication for diagnosing things like broken bones and tumours. This meant that the Warminster hospital, though small, could still rival treatment available at bigger centres.

Susannah died a year later, and true-to-form donated part of her wealth to the benefit of the hospital. She had planned another new wing to the hospital, and even laid the foundation stone of it in 1898, but her will gave more money to the project. She donated £1,000, and a further £4,000 to endow and fit out the new provision with equipment, furniture, beds and so on. This was a vast amount of money at that time, but was only really a drop in the ocean since she left over £36,000 to her executors, who were a bank manager and a solicitor.

The wing, called the Susannah Smith Wing, was opened in August 1899 by the Bishop of Salisbury. There was a ceremony and a tea, and music played by the Warminster Town Band to celebrate.

This benevolence meant that the town hospital had 15 beds to nurse the people of the town, and keep the sick near their loved ones, with various other facilities to treat ailments and illnesses that didn't require inpatient treatment. Though possibly borne from deep religious faith, the kindness of souls like Susannah and Eliza was not endemic for those in their position, and it is clear that they cared deeply about improving conditions for all people across the town, irrespective of class or background.

The wings provided by Susannah and Eliza sadly did not last past the mid-1920s. More beds were needed, with the town expanding, and the buildings were found to be in a poor state. A new hospital was built on the field next door, and the original building with its two 1890s wings was demolished in 1929. The names of the wings, and that of their benefactors, were not preserved in the names of portions of the new hospital, and the contributions of Susannah and Eliza have therefore not been remembered until recently.

References

Bath Chronicle and Weekly Gazette, 20 January 1831, Excellent Cabinet and Chairmakers' Stock

Bath Chronicle, 7 February 1861, Suicide

Bristol Mercury, 10 December 1892, Deaths

Bristol Mercury, 2 August 1899, Warminster

Devizes and Wiltshire Gazette, 2 August 1888, Warminster

England and Wales census collection, held by Ancestry.co.uk

England and Wales Civil Registration Births, Marriages and Deaths, held by Ancestry.co.uk

England & Wales, National Probate Calendar (Index of Wills and Administrations), 1858-1995, held by Ancestry.co.uk

England & Wales, Prerogative Court of Canterbury Wills, 1384-1858, held by Ancestry.co.uk

Friends of Warminster Cottage Hospital, (2023), *History*, at https://fowh.org/history (accessed 13.1.2025)

Index To Death Duty Registers 1796-1903, held by FindMyPast.co.uk

Scotland 1841 Census, held by ScotlandsPeople.co.uk

Scotland 1861 Census, held by ScotlandsPeople.co.uk

Somerset, England, Church of England Baptisms, 1813-1914, held by Ancestry.co.uk

Somerset, England, Church of England Baptisms, Marriages, and Burials, 1531-1812, held by Ancestry.co.uk

Somerset, England, Church of England Burials, 1813-1914, held by Ancestry.co.uk

Somerset, England, Marriage Registers, Bonds and Allegations, 1754-1914, held by Ancestry.co.uk

Somerset Standard, 30 April 1892, Opening of a New Wing of the Cottage Hospital

Trowbridge Chronicle, 4 August 1888, Deaths

UK and Ireland, The Royal National Lifeboat Institution Records, 1824-1989, held by Ancestry.co.uk

UK, Register of Duties Paid for Apprentices' Indentures, 1710-1811, held by Ancestry.co.uk

Warminster & Westbury journal, and Wilts County Advertiser, 28 July 1888, Death of Miss Vicary

Warminster & Westbury journal, and Wilts County Advertiser, 28 March 1891, The Cottage Hospital

Warminster & Westbury journal, and Wilts County Advertiser, 30 April 1892, Warminster Cottage Hospital – Addition of a New Wing: Opening Ceremony

Warminster & Westbury journal, and Wilts County Advertiser, 4 September 1897, Cottage Hospital

Western Gazette, 29 April 1892, The New Wing of the Cottage Hospital

Nobel Prize Outreach (2025). Wilhelm Conrad Röntgen – Biographical, at. https://www.nobelprize.org/prizes/physics/1901/rontgen/biographical/ (accessed 13.1.2025)

Wiltshire Burials Index 1538-1990, held by FindMyPast.co.uk

Wiltshire, England, Church of England Baptisms, Marriages and Burials, 1538-1812, held by Ancestry.co.uk

Wiltshire, England, Church of England Deaths and Burials, 1813-1922, held by Ancestry.co.uk

Wiltshire Memorial Inscription Index, held by FindMyPast.co.uk

Wiltshire Times and Trowbridge Advertiser, 28 July 1888, Warminster: Death of Miss Vicary

Wiltshire Times and Trowbridge Advertiser, 5 August 1899, Warminster

Dorothy May Lodge

IT'S WELL KNOWN that Florence Nightingale was the mother of formalised nursing in the UK. After her experiences during the Crimean War (1853-1856), she established the world's first professional nursing school at St Thomas's Hospital in London, in 1860.

The principles of this school informed the formation of the British National Society for Aid to the Sick and Wounded in War in 1870, which was renamed the British Red Cross in 1905. And, though much nursing continued unregulated and untrained through the rest of the 19th century – first aid and more general care were usually provided in the home by relatives, while for longer term cases a live-in nurse would be employed – this was the start of a trend towards more formalised and trained nursing.

Dorothy Lodge – who came from Winterbourne Earls, a village a little to the north-east of Salisbury, originally – became a district nurse in the 1920s, and by this time nursing was a well-established and desirable job for a young woman, with a clear training path.

Her family were deeply Methodist, and attended the local chapel. She was the youngest of ten children. When she was born in 1895, her father Thomas was a shepherd, and she might just have followed a traditional agricultural pathway for her early life, being educated at the board school, then undertaking jobs on the land before marrying a labourer and raising her family. However, the advent of the 20th century and its changing ambitions and roles for women meant that other ideas were open to women like Dorothy.

Initially, before the First World War, her brothers went into agricultural work, and she followed the traditional route, becoming a domestic servant to a soldier at Amesbury by the time she was 16.

However, with an increased need for medical staff during the war, at the age of 20 Dorothy was training at the Woolwich Union Infirmary in London, as part of the Queen's Nursing Institute – which focussed on nursing in the community. She began this training at the height of the war in November 1916. This was part of a workhouse building – workhouses having offered basic medical care to the local community as part of their remit – but was separately built as a hospital in 1874. From 1902 it had a nurses' home where young women boarded and received training. Dorothy would have moved away from home and into the guidance of a matron, training with many other young women. Her training continued here for just over two years, until January 1920, and she was able to take on a proper nursing job.

Her first proper job was at the Brompton Hospital in London, from February 1920 onwards. Then, as now, it was a specialist hospital for chest and lung complaints, which specialised in consumption and tuberculosis treatment – both common killers at the time that Dorothy trained. She remained there until the autumn, when she moved for a stint at the hospital in Paddington. This again was attached to a workhouse, and had a nurses' home – where Dorothy would have stayed – and a teaching remit. St Mary's Hospital, next door, was where Alexander Flemming discovered penicillin in 1928. All of Dorothy's nursing experiences in London therefore pre-dated the use of this wonder-drug.

She remained at Paddington until May 1921, and attended lectures in social subjects – which would have covered the health around poverty in cities – diseases of the eyes, ears and throat, monthly nursing (looking after a woman before and after birth), women's diseases, and hygiene. She can then be found living in a nurses' home in Tottenham on the 1921 census, alongside other nurses in training, and is known to have also worked at Kilburn and Woolwich hospitals too. She became a fully-fledged nurse, having completed all that training, in July 1923 in London.

She would have been in her mid-20s by this stage, in an era when the common age to marry was around 21. Many young women of her generation lost sweethearts during the war, and this may have been the case for Dorothy. She also may have loved her training and job so much that she did not wish to marry as that would have brought it to an end.

Nursing, as a recognised profession, was subject to a marriage bar at this time. This meant that had Dorothy wanted to get married at any point, she would have been expected to give up her job to do so – no matter how much training she had done or what positions she had held. Nurses were not alone in being subject to a marriage bar, as women teachers and civil servants were also affected, among others. Nominally, the idea behind a marriage bar was to clear the way for new unmarried women to come into the profession by freeing up what was felt to be a finite number of jobs. And married women were felt to have acquired different priorities – a husband, a home, forthcoming children – which would distract them from their work.

In reality though, after the greater working freedoms afforded to women (married as well as single) during the First World War, this marriage bar was often chafed against. Prime Minister Lloyd George's government elected in December 1918 was well aware of this, particularly as employed women were worried they'd lose their jobs to returning soldiers, and passed a piece of legislation in 1919. The Sex Disqualification (Removal) Act passed in December 1919, section one, stated:

> A person shall not be disqualified by sex or marriage from the exercise of any public function, or from being appointed to or holding any civil or judicial office or post, or from entering or assuming or carrying on any civil profession or vocation, or for admission to any incorporated society (whether incorporated by Royal Charter or otherwise), [and a person shall not be exempted by sex or marriage from the liability to serve as a juror]

Effectively, this lifted most common-law or assumed restrictions on women's working, and meant that professions were open to women – magistrates, jurors, justice of the peace, solicitors, for example. At least in theory, it removed the marriage bar from working women.

In practice, however, the Act does not seem to have made much difference outside the governmental and legal spheres. Nurses were still expected to leave their job if they wished to marry.

In 1923, Elizabeth Price – a married infants' school teacher from Clydach Vale, who had been told that her employer Rhondda UDC was enforcing an official marriage bar on their women teachers – tested that legislation. She had long service behind her – 26 years teaching, 21 of them married – and was living proof that a woman could run a house and family and a successful job concurrently. She, and 57 other women in her position, took them to court. Price v. Rhondda Urban District Council went to the Chancery Division of the High Court on 24 April 1923. The action was seen by many as a test case for the 1919 Act, and many organisations employing women awaited its outcome.

The case was heard by Mr Justice Eve – Sir Harry Trelawny Eve, a barrister, judge and Liberal Party politician. He and the court upheld the dismissals in early May, ruling that the Sex Disqualification (Removal) Act merely stated that marriage did not disqualify women from employment, but that it did not mean married women were necessarily entitled to employment.

Many organisations employing women across the country awaited this judgement – including nursing – and Mr Justice Eve's decision rendered the 1919 Act effectively useless. Marriage bars were officially enacted across the board in the wake of this, and the prohibition remained for nurses, including Dorothy. The nurses' register papers had a box for whether the woman was single or a widow – there was not an option for married.

This judgement came as Dorothy was completing her formal nursing training, working at her final placement in Central St Pancras as a minor ailment centre nurse. She stayed here once her training was finished, and was regarded as conscientious and reliable, according to her notes.

Central London was beginning to rise out of the crippling poverty and poor public health that had characterised the area in Victorian and Edwardian times, and Dorothy's nursing work would have put her on the front line of this change. Focusing on the health of mothers and children was at the heart of this. The first birth control clinic had been set up by Marie Stopes in north London in 1921, scandalising many with the very idea, and other clinics were beginning to focus on encouraging better maternal health and fewer pregnancies. This meant that the average size of a family dropped considerably.

Regulating midwifery services again played a part in this, improving both infant and maternal mortality rates. Dorothy decided to add this skill to her nursing too. She attended formal midwifery training at North Middlesex hospital from October 1924 until February 1925, and was certified the following June. After this, she returned to her clinic role at St Pancras.

She stayed there until October 1926, when she decided to resign from the Queen's Nursing Institute to take a position closer to home in Wiltshire. Her final report as she left said that she was an excellent, tactful and conscientious worker, and a pleasant colleague to work with. She had recently turned 30, and her father had died the year before, so she and her siblings were probably looking to rally around to support her mother.

She took a job as a district nurse, based initially in Hurdcott – a touch to the south of Winterbourne Earls, where she'd grown up. The BBC television programme *Call The Midwife* examines the role of district nurses in London in the 1950s as part of its drama, but Dorothy's life and work in 1920s rural Wiltshire was likely to be far more humdrum with a good deal less companionship.

She was based in what was described in the records as The Hut, which may have been a nursing base or the name of her house, and probably nominally attached to nursing services at a nearby hospital – likely Salisbury Infirmary – and part of the 1920-created General Nursing Council (GNC). She would have worn a strict uniform, and worked a high number of hours a week. And she would have travelled the district either by bicycle or car (it's noted that she could drive on her nursing record) dispensing care to people across the local village communities.

Her likely duties would be to provide some first aid, care for and dress existing wounds, dispense the proper dosage for prescribed medicines, spot and provide initial treatment for infectious diseases, and deliver the local babies – as she kept up her role as a midwife too, though that role was administrated through another base in the village of Upper Woodford, a few miles away from Hurdcott.

She would have been responsible for administering drugs like insulin, which was discovered and then used a treatment for diabetics in the early 1920s in Canada, and began to be used more widely in the UK after the first patient was treated at Guy's Hospital in 1925.

Dorothy would also have been on the front line for spotting diseases like polio and tuberculosis in the local population. Still a huge killer in this period, the 1921 Public Health (Tuberculosis) Act meant that councils had to provide sanitoria and aftercare for those suffering, and by 1925 – just before Dorothy arrived back in the area – it became compulsory to isolate sufferers to prevent it spreading. A vaccine, the BCG, became available from 1927, but a cure didn't materialise until after a penicillin-based antibiotic became more widely available around the time of the Second World War.

Though it is hard to search the nursing records effectively, she appears to have been the only district nurse for the village for much of her time there. Occasionally, another younger woman appears in the registers, so she may have been instrumental in training other district nurses rather than taking on a colleague.

Away from her work, her mother and several siblings still lived in and around Winterbourne Earls, and she was also involved in the life of the villages that she served within – there's a reference to her serving teas at a Women's Institute event in Woodford in 1927.

This pattern of life continued until just before the Second World War, when she appears to have moved slightly closer to Amesbury, into the tiny community of Lake. This is a touch further up the River Avon from Upper Woodford, but she still kept up the same job. The 1939 register, taken in September of that year to keep track of the population in wartime, has Dorothy living alone in Riverside Cottage in Lake as a professional nurse. She would have been in her mid-40s, and does not seem to have taken on any additional roles during the conflict.

Though based in Lake, she continued to serve in Hurdcott until at least 1946, then disappears from the nursing registers. Her midwife role in Lake continued however, so she was still responsible for delivering the local youngsters across these villages.

Her mother Mary Ann's 100th birthday celebrations, in September 1955, reported in *Salisbury Times* that Dorothy was still the district nurse at Woodford, so it seems likely that she continued with this vital dual role until her retirement. Indeed, when her mother died in 1958, Dorothy was still being referred to as a district nurse in the newspaper.

Her final mention in official medical registers was in 1959, but that is the last year of them available publicly, so it is always possible that she carried on working after that. At that stage she would have been aged around 64, and retirement age was technically 60, so keeping going would have been unusual.

Not having married, she did not have her own children to spend time with at leisure during her retirement. But, as the youngest of her siblings, she undoubtedly had many nieces and nephews to see and enjoy. As she would have birthed and aided much of the district, she was likely incredibly well-known and very involved in village life and undoubtedly her church too.

She died in 1988, having been living in Hurdcott at a house that had been named for her parents – Stevemary.

References

British Red Cross (2025), The beginning of the Red Cross, at: https://www.redcross.org.uk/about-us/our-history/movement-origin (accessed 8.7.2025)

England & Wales, Civil Registration Birth Index, 1837-1915, held by Ancestry.co.uk

England & Wales, Civil Registration Death Index, 1916-2007, held by Ancestry.co.uk

England & Wales, National Probate Calendar (Index of Wills and Administrations), 1858-1995, held by Ancestry.co.uk

Kelly's Directory of Wiltshire, 1939

Nursing Times (2005), A history of nursing in Britain: the 1920s, at https://www.nursingtimes.net/history-of-nursing/a-history-of-nursing-in-britain-the-1920s-26-08-2021/ (accessed 8.7.2025)

NHS (2025), Royal Brompton Hospital, at https://guysandstthomas.shorthandstories.com/royal-brompton-hospital/index.html (accessed 8.7.2025)

Salisbury Times, 9 September 1927, For Salisbury Infirmary

Salisbury Times, 30 September 1955, Mrs Mary Ann Lodge of Hurdcott

Salisbury Times, 27 September 1957, 102 years old

Salisbury Times, 14 February 1958, Death of Mrs Lodge

UK census collection, held by Ancestry.co.uk

UK & Ireland, Nursing Registers, 1898-1968, held by Ancestry.co.uk

UK & Ireland, Queen's Nursing Institute Roll of Nurses, 1891-1931, held by Ancestry.co.uk

UK, The Midwives Roll, 1904-1959, held by Ancestry.co.uk

Wiltshire, England, Church of England Births and Baptisms, 1813-1922, held by Ancestry.co.uk

Jane Goodfellow or Shore

JANE GOODFELLOW LOST not only her husband when he ran off with a barmaid, but also her own identity when her husband's lover claimed her name on the 1851 census in a vain attempt at respectability. She later brought one of the first civil divorce cases against him, after a new act was passed in 1857 enabling women to do so for the first time.

You could be forgiven for thinking that nothing had happened between Jane and her husband Charles, since she seemingly appears alongside him and their children in West Ham in 1851. However, the actual Jane filed for divorce from Charles in 1858, and says in her paperwork that he'd left her in 1841 – which makes the woman with him in 1851 his lover Elizabeth, and not Jane at all. So, Jane actually appears on that census twice – once fake, and once with information she'd given the enumerator herself.

Jane was born in Fovant in around 1806, and had married Charles Shore in 1828 in Stockton – where she'd moved to during her childhood. Stockton lies close to the River Wylye in Wiltshire, between Warminster and Salisbury, while Fovant sits further south. Both were small rural communities. She is likely the daughter of James Goodfellow, a carpenter who died while she was still quite young, and Rhoda, née Matthews. Her father's death seems to have put the family – mother Rhoda and Jane's siblings Hester, James, John, Mary, Elizabeth and Martha – close to the poverty line, as her mother subsequently gives her occupation as a pauper on early census returns.

Moving over to Stockton and subsequently marrying Charles must have seemed a bit of a step up for Jane. Charles came from Heytesbury, also relatively close by, and his father was a mason. They lived at Stockton for eight years after their marriage, while Charles worked as a farm labourer, and then moved to Trowbridge for him to run a carrying business between that town and Salisbury, and to subsequently run a pub and a business as a carrier – moving goods along roads as haulage.

Much of this detail comes from Jane's divorce petition, submitted in 1858, which fills in a great deal of the back story.

The likely pub premises, as they're roughly where Jane was living on the 1841 census, was the Brewery Tap on Back Street in Trowbridge, now long-since defunct, and probably serving Ushers ales, as the brewery was nearby. In all likelihood, though Charles would have been the landlord and held the licence on paper, it would probably have been Jane that did the day-to-day running of the pub. This situation was relatively common among landlords and landladies of pubs at the time.

The 1841 census, taken around a month after Charles deserted Jane, finds her still in the pub premises, with a new barmaid and a five-year-old girl, also called Jane though bearing Jane's maiden surname. Jane states in her divorce petition that she'd had no children with Charles, so it's likely that the younger Jane was a niece, the daughter of one of her many siblings, who partially fulfilled a child role in the couple. It's relatively common to find niblings being brought up by their aunts – sometimes due to economic necessity, as that would be one less mouth for the parents to feed, but also sometimes passed over to childless couples, perhaps as a kindness in a society where motherhood was seen as a perfect state for women.

When the 1851 census was taken, Jane had given up the pub and had moved to Bath with her niece, where she was making a living as a nurse. This would not have been a nurse in a hospital during this era, but more someone who went into people's houses to care for them if they were sick, or incapacitated after childbirth or an accident. It would have not been the most lucrative profession, but would have given her enough to live on. She more often worked as a monthly nurse. This was someone who cared for a woman in the final stages of pregnancy and through the birth, and lived in different households for a month at a time. She also probably did some of the chores of the household while the woman was lying in – a period of pre- and post-birth time where the new mother was not expected to leave her bed in order to heal properly and be well-rested.

In contrast, Fake Jane, aka Elizabeth, was living with Jane's husband Charles and two children in West Ham, where Charles was working as an engine driver on the railway. In addition to their own two children, Elizabeth had also taken in a nursechild, which meant that she'd probably lost a baby in the preceding year, but had taken in another child who needed her breastmilk. The reason for the deception of Elizabeth using Jane's name on the official document was probably to do with respectability, as she was posing as his wife to all intents and purposes, but they perhaps feared some retribution on a legal document, as the census was. Therefore, she used the name Jane rather than Elizabeth. It's probable that Jane never knew of this deception.

There was a major overhaul in divorce law in parliament in 1857. Until this point, divorce could only be achieved via an act of parliament, and only men could bring proceedings. The change was partly brought about by the campaigning of Caroline Norton, who (finally) received a blue plaque for her efforts in 2021. Later known as Lady Stirling-Maxwell, Caroline had married unsuccessful barrister George Chapple Norton, the MP for Guildford, in 1827. Their marriage was unhappy, and George often possessive and abusive, and she left him in 1836 – but had no legal recompense when he claimed her earnings as his own, and abducted their children. Caroline thereafter was involved in campaigning for more rights for women and children, writing to Queen Victoria on the matter, and when Parliament debated divorce reform in 1855 she submitted an account of her marriage as evidence.

The Matrimonial Causes Act 1857 brought divorce into the civil courts, and out of the realms of the church. It also meant that for the first time women could bring divorce proceedings, or seek ways out of the legal trappings of a marriage, which is more what Caroline Norton wanted. And this enabled Jane to seek recompense for what had happened to her.

Jane's plea for divorce, filed on 8th November 1858, was only the second divorce case from Wiltshire under the new 1857 act, (the first was Amelia Willett, in February 1858), and was a straight plea for the marriage to end.

Under the Act, which came into force on 1 January 1858, men could achieve a divorce by just proving their wife had had an affair. Women had to prove their husband's adultery, in addition to something else he'd done wrong: either extreme cruelty, desertion, bigamy or incest. Marriages were also ended by nullity – in most cases a previous marriage which had been 'forgotten' to be declared, but occasionally impotence. The Divorce and Matrimonial Court didn't just hear the ends of marriages either – either party could apply for a judicial separation, which mean that they were still legally married, but didn't have to live together. This was often used by women who couldn't prove adultery but wanted to avoid flying fists. Either party could also petition the court under the act for restoration of conjugal rights, therefore forcing their partner to live with them again.

Women could also apply to protect any independent earnings they'd made since their husband's desertion, and the first of the two earliest Wiltshire cases was one of these, filed by Amelia Willett (née Philpott) of Market Lavington in late February 1858.

Jane went to London, to enable her case to be heard in court. The only court able to hear the case was the Court of Chancery, at Westminster Hall. She took lodgings in Southampton Street, and engaged a firm of solicitors from Cheapside.

Jane's story, from the case files, was a straight plea for the marriage to end on the grounds of adultery and desertion. She says that he ran off with the barmaid Elizabeth Doughty and went to live in Vauxhall, where she passed as his wife. He hadn't contributed anything to Jane's upkeep since. She had discovered that they'd lived under the surname Grant, and they'd run an eating house together, but had subsequently moved to Portsmouth.

The case, which was uncontested by Charles, was sent for trial in December, and the minutes were filed in May 1859. There is no definite sign of the verdict in the files, but the London *Morning Herald* reports that July that the divorce was granted. This was probably not before time, as it would have been very easy for her to have run out of money to remain in London and pursue the claim – divorce could be expensive, particularly before the verdict, as the claimant would have had to have funded the proceedings themselves before any costs were awarded in judgement.

The time the legal proceedings took – other divorce papers have lawyer's lackeys sent to hunt down the defendants, to get their answers to the divorce petitions – may mean that they were unable to find Charles in order to answer the summons. If Charles and Elizabeth called themselves Grant, that they were unable to be found.

After her victory, Jane returned to her previous nursing life. The 1861 census has her caring for the rector's wife in Dunkerton, Somerset, a bit south of Bath, who had a month-old baby. Ten years later, the 1871 census has her visiting a friend on Conigre in Trowbridge, round the corner from her former pub, though she was still working as a nurse.

After that she disappears from view, and probably was mis-recorded in her death record as she would most likely have been living in someone else's house when death occurred and they would not have had her full details to bury her properly. Someone bearing her name was buried in Bishop's Lavington, now West Lavington, in 1884, but this would appear to be someone else who had lived there for years and not the Jane we are looking for. It is always possible that she had married again, but there is no record to bear this theory out either.

Charles and Elizabeth never seem to have married, however, which could mean that Charles was never told of the success of Jane's divorce petition. Elizabeth Doughty might have pretended to be Jane on the 1851 census, but used her own name afterwards. She and Charles had at least five daughters together, and moved to Portsmouth where Charles still worked as a railway engine driver. He later ran a horse drawn taxi cab around Portsmouth, but he appears to have stayed faithful to Elizabeth for the rest of his life. He died in Portsea Island in 1881.

The humble professions of Charles and Jane should hopefully help to dispel the idea that divorce in this period was a preserve of the rich. They certainly weren't. Jane would have saved enough money from her work to afford the legal fees, while waiting for the legislation to be put in place for her divorce case to be heard. Pauper cases were also heard, although they were rarer.

Without the information given in the legal files, a very different picture of this couple could have emerged. We would have had no way of discerning what had caused the split, and could have thought Jane had gone to Vauxhall with Charles, since Elizabeth used her name. Her divorce case gives her back her truth and her history.

References

BBC, History: Caroline Norton, at https://www.bbc.co.uk/history/historic_figures/norton_caroline.shtml (accessed 1.9.2024)

Carlisle Journal, 26 August 1853, Caroline Norton

England and Wales 1921 census, held by Findmypast.co.uk

England & Wales, Civil Divorce Records, 1858-1918, held by Ancestry.co.uk

England & Wales, Civil Registration Birth Index, 1837-1915, held by Ancestry.co.uk

England & Wales, Civil Registration Marriage Index, 1837-1915, held by Ancestry.co.uk

England & Wales, Civil Registration Death Index, 1835-1915, held by Ancestry.co.uk

Man of Ross and General Advertiser, 21 January 1858, The New Divorce Act

Morning Herald (London), 6 June 1838, The Honourable Mrs Caroline Norton

Morning Herald (London), 11 July 1859, Shore v. Shore

UK Census collection, held by Ancestry.co.uk

Wiltshire, England, Church of England Births and Baptisms, 1813-1922, held by Ancestry.co.uk

Wiltshire, England, Church of England Marriages and Banns, 1754-1916, held by Ancestry.co.uk

Wiltshire, England, Church of England Deaths and Burials, 1813-1922 held by Ancestry.co.uk

Wiltshire, England, Marriages, 1538-1837, held by Ancestry.co.uk

Thirza Newman, Harriet Judd or Sutton, and friends

THIRZA NEWMAN AND Harriet Judd almost certainly never met. What brings their stories together is that their job descriptions have been similarly recorded in official records: prostitute.

However, while Harriet – who came from Salisbury – was almost certainly a sex worker during the early 1850s, Manningford-Abbots-born Thirza seems to have been more of an immoral character in the eyes of Victorian society, and instead had that assumption thrust upon her by the people who surrounded her.

Both came from working class labouring backgrounds. Harriet, born in 1831, grew up around town industries, which her parents George and Sophia would have laboured within. Thirza, born in the summer of 1848, had a far more rural background, and her father Thomas and mother Maria would have worked in agricultural settings.

They would have grown up expecting to go into those workplaces themselves, but something seems to have thrown them off the expected track. For Harriet, that was probably the early death of her father – he'd gone by the time she was eight years old, leaving her mother to bring up Harriet and her three younger siblings – and a bout of mental illness that occurred when she was around 18. Thirza instead seems to have been living on the poverty line, coupled with not caring a jot about what was considered right and proper around behaviour for a young woman, and she chafed against expectations.

When it comes to sex work, however, Harriet is known to have been a 'common prostitute', by its very definition under the Vagrancy Act 1824 someone who regularly engaged in selling sexual acts, and is reported upon as such in both newspaper reports and the 1851 census. Thirza, though called a prostitute on her criminal record, and on the 1871 census when she was in prison, does not appear to have ever been charged with soliciting. Instead, in her case, the assumption of prostitution seems to have been derived from the fact that she'd fallen from the good path that society felt she ought to trodden, and her looser morals meant that she was therefore a prostitute rather than branded a 'common prostitute'.

Harriet seems to have been particularly active in the underbelly of Salisbury society around 1850 to 1853. There's a reference in the *Salisbury and Winchester Journal* of November 1850 to her and two other women – Maria Gale and Mary Ann Amor – being charged with being common prostitutes. Harriet received a prison sentence of 14 days, while her companions got seven days apiece. This was probably served at the Fisherton gaol, which at that time was located at the junction of Devizes and Wilton Roads in what is now central Salisbury. This had 96 cells, with provision for women prisoners, and Harriet and her companions would have been under the care of the matron. Though not stated, the sentence probably involved hard labour – likely a pointless physical activity – and some sort of work activity like laundry or sewing. There would have also been daily religious instruction to attempt to bring the women back to the right path.

It does not appear to have worked. Harriet and Mary Ann Amor can be found four months later on the 1851 census in a house on Bedwin Street, Salisbury, again referred to as 'common prostitutes'. They were both 19, and each seems to have had their own quarters in the house. Head of the household was 25-year-old Maria Curtis, not the same person as Maria Gale – who was younger and elsewhere at that time – who had an unknown male guest in the house that night. He, perhaps wisely, was never given a name by either the women or the census enumerators, being referred to as a stranger of about 20 years old, and his birthplace unknown.

There is no further record of Maria Curtis, as she perhaps didn't give her correct name to the authorities. Maria Gale, their erstwhile companion, pops up a couple more times in courts and newspapers for unseemly behaviour in the streets, but no more links to sex work. She eventually had an illegitimate daughter, took her father to court for support, married another man, and died young.

Harriet and Mary Ann Amor continue to pop up as sex workers and criminals for a few more years.

In October 1851, Harriet was up in front of the court again. She had apparently made a male acquaintance, George Spender, who had accompanied her to a 'house of ill fame' on Winchester Street in

Salisbury, not too far from the one on Bedwin Street she'd been at before. While there, she'd stolen a purse from him, containing a bank note for £5, three sovereigns and a five-shilling coin. Harriet's defence was that he'd given her the money, but the jury took George's side, and she received a year's prison sentence with hard labour, to be served at Fisherton Anger. The matron's journal reports that in February 1852, while serving this sentence, Harriet had been disorderly at a chapel service and had used bad language. She was sent to solitary confinement.

Meanwhile, while Harriet was in prison, her friend Mary Ann Amor was still at large. She was brought before the court in April 1852, described by the *Wiltshire County Mirror* as 'a young woman of repulsive appearance'. Apparently, she'd created 'a most disgraceful disturbance at a brothel in Bedwin Street', while being drunk and disorderly, which had been kept up from 7pm until 1am the previous Saturday night. In addition, she'd had a man who'd been in the street with her beaten by two other men, and thrown into the refuse channel that ran up the middle of the road. She had to pay £10 to the magistrates to keep the peace. She seems to have paid the fine, which indicates that her business was doing well.

A year or so later, Mary Ann caused another disturbance in the Salisbury streets, this time with another woman – Hester Alderman. She was charged with prostitution and having used obscene language, and received a further three-week spell in Fisherton Anger gaol. Notably, Harriet was not with her this time. And after this, Mary Ann Amor disappears from all available records completely. She may have moved away, or gone by an alias afterwards. The house in Bedwin Street, which had housed Harriet, Maria and Mary Ann on the 1851 census, was due to be indicted at the next Quarter Sessions by residents who wanted the trade moved on.

In contrast, Thirza's journey along a path her society disapproved of seems far less riotous and instead initially borne out of sheer necessity for survival. As one of seven children living in a tiny cottage, supported by one agricultural labourer's wage, existence was probably very much hand-to-mouth, with children expected to earn as soon as they were able.

Thirza's first brush with the law came in July 1861, when she was around 13, and was against this background. She stole a quantity of potatoes from a field near Pewsey, some from George Usher and some from William White. They were probably just as much on the poverty line as Thirza and her family, and Thirza's motivation would almost certainly have been hunger, but the law was the law. She received 14 days imprisonment with hard labour for each charge, so would have spent a month in Devizes New Bridewell Prison.

Prison was then, as now, supposed to be a deterrent to continuing criminal behaviour. But having been convicted of a crime and spending time in gaol carried a huge societal stigma at this time, and many would just have assumed that Thirza was a wrong'un, no matter what she did next.

What she did next was to play up to the bar, and the deterrent of being under lock and key with hard labour did not work in her case. It may be that being in a secure environment with regular food was better than being at home, and this could have been a motivation of sorts. It was not unheard of for women to deliberately commit minor criminal acts – for example, deliberately swearing outside a police station - in order to procure a safe bed for a period of time, this being more secure than fending for themselves.

Thirza, in March 1862 when she was around 14, damaged the local vicar's ash trees and those belonging to another parishioner too. She received another two 14-day sentences. Then in October 1864, at 16-ish, she was charged with stealing 25 herrings from a fish hawker, and a basket full of clothes and other oddments from another hawker at the same time. Both were found in her house, though the herrings couldn't be satisfactorily identified so that charge was dropped. For this, she received six months at Devizes prison.

At the same time, her father Thomas was investigated for stealing a couple of bushels of potatoes, which were found at the same time as the baskets that Thirza had stolen. He declared no knowledge of them whatsoever, so the investigation was dropped – and may well have been put there by Thirza herself or another of her siblings. Thirza may well have stolen a great deal more than we are able to hear about through documents, as official papers only record what she was charged with when found out.

Nowhere, in any of these reports and convictions, is there any indication that Thirza was selling sex for money or food – like Harriet had very clearly been doing a decade earlier in Salisbury. But when she is put into the prison system, Thirza is being branded as a prostitute, rather than a thief as she actually appears to have been. This may have been a judgement on behalf of the management of Devizes prison at the time, as many women who came through the doors seem to be routinely branded as prostitutes whatever their crime. It could be a blanket judgement from those who kept the records that every woman not on the good and godly path was therefore a prostitute. Some record takers would do this – H S Plumptie, a vicar in the Cowbridge area of South Wales in the earlier 19th century, would regularly record unmarried women as a 'strumpet' on her illegitimate child's baptism (unless they were in service to the father, in which case they were a servant – but unusually for the time did write down the name of both parents in each case).

Again, six months inside does not seem to have cowed Thirza into the sort of woman that society expected her to be. In October 1865 there is a report in the *Wiltshire County Mirror* that she, along with Mary Strong and Martha Wiltshire of Pewsey, had been charged with being drunk and fighting on the streets of Pewsey that September. They were each fined £2 and the costs of the legal action, but because they couldn't afford it they were taken by cart to Fisherton Anger gaol. Thirza and friends reportedly sang 'Slap Bang, here we are again' as the conveyance left.

Later that same year, she was acquitted of stealing 2s 7½d, from Sidney Herbert Strong in Pewsey.

However, the punishments were starting to step up, and Thirza's previous convictions were adding to the length of time she spent inside with each offence. Stealing 1 ¼ pounds of bacon in Manningford Abbots in April 1866 got her another six months, taking into account her previous crimes. She was described as 19 years old, and a labourer.

In September 1868 she received another three weeks for indecent behaviour in church. It appears that she'd been ushered into the pew by the parish clerk, where she'd made 'improper noises', and when he told her to stop it she'd spat in his face. This was added to her now considerable record. She also had to pay damages for damaging the underwood of Sir Francis Dugdale Astley at Manningford Abbots at around the same time.

The final straw appears to have come in November 1868, when Thirza and a friend – Elizabeth Edwards, described by the *Devizes and Wiltshire Gazette* as 'two impudent young women' – stole two cloaks from Mr Fremlin's shop in Long Street, Devizes. They were pursued by a man who lived opposite, and committed for trial at the Borough Quarter Sessions, which were due to be held in early January 1869. At the ensuing trial, Thirza – because of her litany of previous convictions – was handed a sentence of seven years penal servitude.

Transportation to the colonies for penal servitude had ended 16 years earlier, in 1853, so Thirza was committed to Fisherton Anger gaol for her seven years. However, that prison was in the process of shutting down around then, so by August 1869 she had been moved to Woking Female Prison in Surrey, which had opened that April. Here, as it was a specialist women's facility, she would not have undergone traditional hard labour outside. She would likely have spent a long time in her cell, and worked in the prison kitchens and laundry, or on the prison farm. There was also emphasis on worship in the prison chapel. The prison could cope with up to 700 women at a time, though when Thirza arrived it would have been below that capacity.

Thirza seems to have been relatively well behaved at Woking. Quarterly reports of her conduct throughout 1870 and 1871 say that she was healthy, and exhibiting either good or very good behaviour. The 1871 census was taken while she was there, and it is on that record that she was officially declared a prostitute. More official prison records just make reference to her larceny and previous convictions, and it is possibly no coincidence that there are several other prostitutes listed among the inmates.

However, a change occurs in December 1872. Thirza's behaviour had altered, and she was removed from Woking and sent to Millbank prison instead. Millbank sat where the Tate Britain Gallery now stands, in London. Millbank had a female facility, and many women were sent there from Woking for solitary confinement, so it is possible that there was one disobedient act from Thirza that had facilitated this change. At Millbank, the quarterly conduct reports record that her behaviour was indifferent, and her health unsound.

Lunacy patients admission records reveal that Thirza was under the care of Broadmoor asylum prison – where mentally ill criminals were housed – even if she was incarcerated at Millbank. This indicates that her change in behaviour and status was down to a period of mental instability. She was referred to as indifferent and unsound at Millbank for much of 1873, but began to convalesce by the autumn, and was returned to full care of Millbank that December.

In January 1874, she seems to have been given a licensed release, after serving five years of her seven-year sentence. After that, like Mary Ann Amor a decade or so earlier, Thirza completely disappears from the records. She would have been around 26 years old. There is no marriage or death record for her after that, nor a census entry, which implies that she may have gone by an alias thereafter – which meant, if she continued committing crimes, she wasn't beholden to her previous criminal record. There is a possibility of a marriage for her in Swindon, in the 1890s, but this doesn't seem to ring true.

Meanwhile, unlike Thirza and Mary Ann Amor, Harriet Judd had gone straight. She'd taken up with William Sutton, a Salisbury shoemaker with a criminal background (though not as colourful as her own – he'd got a bit of time for stealing tobacco from his employer in the 1840s, and had been cleared of handling counterfeit coin at the same time as one of Harriet's trials), and had a couple of daughters – Fanny and Rosina. On the 1861 census she posed as his wife, though she actually wasn't.

They actually married in 1864, in St Edmund's Church in Salisbury. This was on Bedwin Street, a stone's throw from the former brothel. Harriet was unable to sign her own name, so put a mark. She does not appear to have completely reformed though, as she was charged with another woman – Ann Norris – with being drunk and fighting in Salt Lane in July 1869. She received a fine rather than a prison sentence, and continued to live at home with her husband and daughters. William Sutton, however, was involved in stealing brandy in 1872, and had a month in prison.

Their second daughter, Rosina, was baptised in 1877, at the age of 15, on a day of innocents – indicating far more respect for religion and society on Harriet's part than she'd exhibited previously. The family were living on Pennyfarthing Street at that time, and they spent the next couple of decades living in low quality court housing, which would not have been salubrious but was at least considered decent living. William still made a living as a shoemaker, and Harriet probably joined him in that work but was unacknowledged.

William died in 1894, at White's Court. Harriet went to live at George Street with her daughter Rosina. She eventually ended up at the workhouse, probably because she couldn't afford any other medical care, and died there in 1905.

Neither of her daughters followed her into her former profession. Both married very respectably, Fanny to a boiler maker and Rosina to a haulage contractor, in 1890.

References

Devizes Advertiser, 20 March 1862, Courts
Devizes Advertiser, 6 October 1864, Committed to the New Prison, Devizes
Devizes Advertiser, 1 October 1868, Committed to the New Prison, Devizes
Devizes and Wiltshire Gazette, 5 April 1866, Thirza Newman
Devizes and Wiltshire Gazette, 3 December 1868, Borough Petty Sessions
England and Wales, Births, Marriages and Deaths indexes, held by Ancestry.co.uk
England and Wales Census Collection, held by Ancestry.co.uk
England & Wales, Criminal Registers, 1791-1892, held by Ancestry.co.uk
Glamorganshire, Wales, Anglican Baptisms, Marriages and Burials, 1570-1994, held by Ancestry.co.uk
Hampshire Advertiser, 4 October 1851, Salisbury Police Courts
Hampshire Advertiser, 18 October 1851, Harriet Judd
Moody, F and Nash, R, (2025) *The New Fisherton Gaol*, at https://fishertonhistorysociety.org/the-new-fisherton-gaol/ (accessed 10.1.2025)
Robinson, F.W. (1889), *Female Convict Life at Woking*, at https://www.theprison.org.uk/WokingFemale/life1.shtml (accessed 11.1.2025)
Salisbury and Winchester Journal, 24 October 1846, Nine months
Salisbury and Winchester Journal, 16 November 1850, Committed to the County Gaol
Salisbury and Winchester Journal, 4 October 1851, City Petty Sessions
Salisbury and Winchester Journal, 28 June 1851, Committed to the County Gaol, Salisbury
Salisbury and Winchester Journal, 17 April 1852, Mary Ann Amor
Salisbury and Winchester Journal, 27 August 1853, At the City Police Court
Salisbury and Winchester Journal and General Advertiser, 19 September 1868, Indecent Conduct at Church

Salisbury and Winchester Journal, 3 July 1869, Drunk and Disorderly Conduct
UK, Calendar of Prisoners, 1868-1929, held by Ancestry.co.uk
UK, Criminal Records, 1780-1871, held by Ancestry.co.uk
UK, Lunacy Patients Admission Registers, 1846-1921, held by Ancestry.co.uk
UK, Prison Registers and Statistical Returns 1865-1874, held by Ancestry.co.uk
UK, Quarterly Returns of Prisoners in Convict Prisons/Lunatic Asylums 1869, held by Ancestry.co.uk
Western Gazette, 12 January 1866, Courts
Wiltshire, England, Church of England Births and Baptisms, 1813-1922, held by Ancestry.co.uk
Wiltshire, England, Church of England Deaths and Burials, 1813-1922, held by Ancestry.co.uk
Wiltshire, England, Church of England Marriages and Banns, 1754-1916, held by Ancestry.co.uk
Wiltshire County Mirror, 13 April 1852, A Disreputable Character
Wiltshire County Mirror, 12 July 1853, City Petty Sessions
Wiltshire County Mirror, 31 July 1861, Everley Petty Sessions
Wiltshire County Mirror, 5 October 1864, Courts
Wiltshire County Mirror, 4 October 1865, Courts
Wiltshire County Mirror, 21 May 1872, Salisbury Petty Sessions
Wilts and Gloucestershire Standard, 7 April 1866, Pleaded guilty
Wiltshire Independent, 16 February 1854, Courts
Wiltshire Independent, 16 September 1868, Pewsey
Wiltshire Social & Institutional Records 1123 – 1968, held by FindMyPast.co.uk
Yates, D (2020), *Woking Female Prison, 1869-1895*, for The Institutional History Society, at https://institutionalhistory.com/homepage/prisons/major-prisons/woking-female-prison-1869-1895 (accessed 11.1.2025)

Ellen Pengelly or Yipsing

E LLEN PENGELLY SEEMS to have had a taste for the exotic. At least when it came to her men.

Born to a rural labouring family in Devon, she might have expected to spend her whole life in that county. Instead, she took up with a Japanese-born tea shop owner, found herself in Wiltshire with him for many years, and eventually ended up in London.

But this journey wasn't all plain sailing, as there was heartbreak and considerable deceit along the way, some of which Ellen may not have known herself.

The second child of a farm labourer, she was born in 1867 in Coryton, a tiny hamlet just off the west edge of Dartmoor. She had an older sister, Rosina, and then a clutch of younger siblings. Her mother Elizabeth had fourteen children in all, but only 10 survived to adulthood. Her father John moved the family a few miles away to another tiny community, Marystow, during Ellen's childhood, and the family lived in a cottage close to a sawmill.

Somewhere along the line, while the younger members of the family were settled in rural Devon, both Ellen and her sister Rosina developed more of a sense of adventure. Older sister Rosina went to London and married a railway porter six years her junior in 1891. Ellen, meanwhile, appears to have found employment in the 1880s in the seaside town of Dawlish, just down the Devon coast from Exeter.

Dawlish at that time was considerably more cosmopolitan than tiny rural Devonshire hamlets. The Victorian seaside resort was quite a pinnacle of high fashion and society, as many gentry and upper-class families would take residence in the town for months in high season, and bring their expectations of lifestyle and entertainment with them. Fashionable and full of tourists keen on the benefits of sea bathing (the Ladies Bathing Pavilion had opened in 1880), it's unclear exactly what job Ellen must have taken in the town. Statistically, she was likely to have been a domestic servant of some degree, but the thriving tourist trade and businesses in the area may have meant that she had wider employment opportunities.

One of these businesses belonged to Lock Kie, sometimes Anglicised as Leonard, who became Ellen's man from at least around the autumn of 1889.

Lock Kie Yipsing was the keeper of a short-lived Chinese tea shop in Dawlish, operating so briefly that it is not mentioned in any trade directory of the town. Though actually from Kobe in Japan, he appears to have pretended to be from Hong Kong for authenticity in his business. Exactly how he came to the UK from Japan initially remains a mystery, but he must have had enough capital in the country to be able to found the tea shop.

Tea, mostly imported from India, was deeply ingrained in culture and society in the Victorian age. It was freely drunk across the classes, albeit with different accoutrements and rituals around serving. Chinese tea drinking, however, was a touch above the usual tea shops of the era, with far more eastern exotic mystery and ritual than other fancy establishments, and it is possible that this was where Ellen met Lock Kie – whether she was working the tables there, or passing on business for her employers.

Rather than a marriage, which would have been the more conventional way round of doing things, the first evidence of their relationship in the records is the birth of a son – Leonard Lockkie Yipsing – in Dawlish in the July of 1890. His birth record is that of a legitimate child, meaning that Ellen and Lock Kie had convinced the authorities that they were married even if they weren't.

They had him baptised in Dawlish that December, but by that stage Lock Kie had moved on to a new job as a gentleman's servant in south Wiltshire, and Ellen and Leonard had joined him.

The 1891 census finds the new family in a cottage in the grounds of Hurdcott House, in Barford St Martin – a small village about six miles to the west of Salisbury. Lock Kie's job was the butler for the big house, and Ellen and Leonard were his entourage.

While a Japanese-pretending-to-be-Chinese butler may seem a slightly unusual choice for the British upper classes in the early 1890s, Lock Kie's employment at Hurdcott House makes sense when the resident of the house at that time is revealed. He was John Henry Leech, son of a wealthy merchant, who specialised in entomology (the study of insects) and had travelled extensively in China, Japan and Kashmir. He therefore had a better understanding of far eastern culture and people than many in his circles. Studying insects in their natural habitats would have involved far more interactions with eastern cultures than trading for goods or visiting colonies, and he would have been more understanding of cultural differences than much of the British population at that time. It is possible that Henry Leech and his American wife Nellie met Lock Kie and Ellen while they were on holiday in Devon.

However, it appears that the job at Hurdcott House was short-lived. By the time Ellen gave birth to their next child, son William, in the April of 1892, Lock Kie had taken a new butler job in Bemerton. This village, on the outskirts of Salisbury, did not have any properties grand enough to employ a butler save Bemerton Lodge – so this was likely Lock Kie's new workplace. He, Ellen and their two sons set up home in a cottage nearby on the Wilton Road.

It was here that Ellen seemed to find her feet in Wiltshire. She somehow acquired property in her own name, a prospect that would have seemed far-fetched while growing up in Devon, and this may be testament to her local connections or the amount that Lock Kie was being paid. She owned two cottages in Fugglestone St Peter, given as landlord Mrs Yipsing, and collected rent in 1893 and 1894. This extra income would undoubtedly have been useful for the family, but also gave her a degree of financial independence.

Lock Kie's employer at Bemerton Lodge would have been Dr William Corbin Finch, who owned the private mental asylum Fisherton House. This institution took in patients with mental health issues from across the south west of the UK, and was an alternative to the county asylum system if you could afford it. Whether the care at Fisherton House was any better than that offered at the Wiltshire County Asylum at Roundway in Devizes is open to question, when Victorian understanding of mental illness was basic at best, but Finch's patients were probably more comfortably housed, and had the benefit of Finch being a leading authority on mental illness.

Dr Finch had moved over to Bemerton from his previous house in Fugglestone St Peter in the early 1890s, and it may be that Ellen acquired her two properties in that village from her connection to him. Though they were hers initially, Lock Kie was given as landlord in 1895 and 1900.

She and Lock Kie had a daughter, Ellen, in late 1893, but – in common with many parents at that time – lost her at nine weeks old. Ellen's life with her two sons and Lock Kie therefore probably continued quietly at Bemerton. In that small and semi-rural world, despite the growth of the area, her sons and husband would almost certainly have faced a degree of racism, whether they recognised it as such or not. Her sons would have looked slightly different to the other children in the village, and – whether he was saying he was Japanese or Chinese – Lock Kie's origins might have been viewed with some suspicion. Ellen, who was white, may also have been viewed differently for who she had married. However, this is pure speculation based on known society at the time, and there is no way of knowing if this was their actual experience.

At some point before November 1896, Lock Kie left for a trip to Cape Town in South Africa. He arrived back in Southampton at the end of the year. The purpose of his trip isn't obvious from the shipping records, and no profession is given for him there. He may have gone on business for Dr Finch, or to further his own business interests – assets like land being easier to require in British African colonies than the UK. Ellen and their two sons were left at Bemerton during his absence.

After he arrived back, Ellen had a third son with him – Percy – in November 1898. The final record of Lock Kie in Wiltshire are the electoral registers giving him as the landlord of the properties at Fugglestone St Peter in 1900. And Ellen and the children are alone at Bemerton on the 1901 census, without any visible means of support. Presumably, if Lock Kie had again travelled to South Africa, he was still maintaining his family at home – whether he was still employed by Dr Finch or not.

It is at this point, however, that things began to unravel.

Dr Finch died in 1905, but it is unlikely that Lock Kie was working for him by that time. His next appearance in the records is on the birth record of another son, also called Leonard. This would normally indicate that that his first son named Leonard, who he had had with Ellen, had died, and that the couple were naming their next son in his memory. Instead, the first Leonard was still alive and kicking, and this new Leonard was born to Lock Kie and his wife May. In London.

Again, this would normally perhaps indicate that the first wife, Ellen, had died. But she was still alive too.

What had actually happened was that Lock Kie had taken a new job in London, and at the same time taken up with a new woman – May Samuelson – who he again hadn't married. She later claimed to have married him in about 1901. New son Leonard, known to the world as Toko, was born in May 1904, so Lock Kie must have been involved with May from at least September 1903. What isn't clear from the records is whether Ellen and their three sons had come to London with him by this stage or not. They could well have still been in Wiltshire.

Lock Kie's new job was as a valet for South African financier David John Pullinger, who lived with his wife Ena and children in the rather prestigious Moray Lodge at Campden Hill in Kensington. This was one of seven large and grand houses built in the early 19th century by John Tasker, close to Holland House, and had previously been the residence of silk mercer Arthur James and Kate Lewis, who were the grandparents of actor Sir John Gielgud, and also of New York publisher Joseph Pulitzer. Lock Kie's official residence was the entrance lodge to the house, and he's given as resident there from 1905 onwards, but also maintained a house with May, first on Guildford Street in St Pancras and later on Balfour Road in Wimbledon, then Burnley Road in Stockwell.

It is unknown whether Ellen and May knew about each other being in Lock Kie's life. Given they were initially living in two separate places, it is easy to suppose that they did not, at least initially, but maintaining two families where neither of the two women worked must have been quite a drain on Lock Kie's resources.

In the spring of 1906, Lock Kie and May had a daughter, Geisha, also in London. Again, it is uncertain whether Ellen was in London or Wiltshire at this time. Then, in late 1906, Lock Kie turns up in American records, crossing the border from Mexico into Arizona and heading for New York and then back to London. Quite what he was doing in Mexico and the USA isn't obvious. He admitted to being Japanese in this record, and said he was working as a valet, so he may have been on business for David Pullinger.

Ellen and her sons must have been resident in London by September 1907, as she gave birth to her fifth (fourth surviving) child Francis, known as Frank, at that time. Frank is referred to in the records as the son of Lock Kie, but used a different surname later in life and – given the situation with Lock Kie's other family – may have been from a subsequent relationship that Ellen was having after a split. His total lack of birth record would seem to support this idea, and this would seem to indicate that Lock Kie's two families were more above board than it appears on paper.

To that end, Lock Kie and May had another daughter, Yosan, in the spring of 1910. She can be seen on the 1911 census with mother May and her siblings at a house in Stockwell. That household also took in performers as boarders – there was a burlesque artist and a comedian staying there on census night in 1911. Despite any possible break up, Lock Kie was with his first family, who were living in his work lodgings at Moray Lodge, so the whole family had eventually come to join him in London, not just Ellen.

Round about this time, Ellen began to ail, having picked up pulmonary tuberculosis from somewhere. This would have involved a persistent chronic cough, alongside chest pain and fatigue, night sweats and probably weight loss too. She and her sons moved from the entrance lodge of Moray Lodge to 65 Abingdon Villas, a tall town house in a smart part of Kensington, a few minutes' walk away from Lock Kie's work. He was included on electoral registers there, but may well have lived at work or with May.

Lock Kie and May's daughter Yosan died in the summer of 1911, aged just over a year.

Ellen died in November 1912, at the Kensington town house, having been suffering her ill health for about 18 months. She was 45. She died as Ellen Yipsing, certified by eldest son Leonard, but her probate record used her original surname Pengelly as she wasn't married. She left just over £92, with her widowed mother as executor.

After her death, her sons gradually all stopped using the Yipsing surname, with many of them taking up the name Pengelly instead.

Having stopped working for David Pullinger, Lock Kie went for British citizenship in 1913, saying that he was married to May (but wasn't), and went on the record that he was born in Japan and not China. He and May had another daughter, Yoland, that year too. They finally married in 1931, but he seems to have spent most of his time farming in South Africa from the First World War onwards, and not really around to support his second family, who continued to live in London. He probably died in South Africa in the later 1930s. Moray Lodge, where he had worked, was demolished in the mid-1950s, and Holland Park School now stands on the site.

References

Board Of Trade: Commercial And Statistical Department And Successors: Outwards Passenger Lists, held by FindMyPast.co.uk
Devon, England, Church of England Births and Baptisms, 1813-1920, held by Ancestry.co.uk
Electoral registers 1832-1932, held by FindMyPast.co.uk
England and Wales 1921 census, held by Findmypast.co.uk
England & Wales, Christening Index, 15300-1980, held by Ancestry.co.uk
England & Wales, Civil Registration Birth Index, 1837-1915, held by Ancestry.co.uk
England & Wales, Civil Registration Death Index, 1916-2007, held by Ancestry.co.uk
England & Wales, Civil Registration Marriage Index, 1837-1915, held by Ancestry.co.uk
Hendon & Finchley Times, 18 December 1896, A Tea-Shop in China
London, England, Church of England Marriages and Banns, 1754-1940, held by Ancestry.co.uk
London, England, City Directories, 1736-1943, held by Ancestry.co.uk
London, England, Electoral Registers, 1832-1972, held by Ancestry.co.uk
Surrey, England, Electoral Registers, 1832-1962, held by Ancestry.co.uk
Totnes Weekly Times, 11 February 1888, Dawlish
UK Census Collection, held by Ancestry.co.uk
UK and Ireland, Incoming Passenger Lists, 1878-1960, held by Ancestry.co.uk
UK, Naturalisation Certificates and Declarations, 1870-1916, held by Ancestry.co.uk
U.S., Border Crossings from Mexico to U.S., 1895-1964, held by Ancestry.co.uk
Walker, D (2014) *A little bit of faded grandeur – country life in Kensington*, at The Library Time Machine, at https://rbkclocalstudies.wordpress.com/2014/11/27/a-little-bit-of-faded-grandeur-country-life-in-kensington/ (accessed 15.5.2025)
Whiteaway, T (c2000), *The history of Dawlish*, at http://www.dawlishhistory.org.

uk/historyTW.html (accessed 15.5.2025)

Wiltshire, England, Church of England Births and Baptisms, 1813-1922, held by Ancestry.co.uk

Wiltshire, England, Church of England Deaths and Burials, 1813-1922, held by Ancestry.co.uk

Wiltshire, England, Church of England Marriages and Banns, 1754-1916, held by Ancestry.co.uk

Bessie Gramlick or McClintock

THE NAME 'MISS B Gramlich' is given as a co-chair of the West Wiltshire WSPU (Women's Social and Political Union – the political arm of the movement popularly known as the suffragettes), alongside that of Lillian Dove-Willcox (a prominent active WSPU member known to have frequented Trowbridge from Bristol around that time) in 1911-12.

Miss B Gramlich would appear to be Elizabeth Gramlick, known as Bessie, one of several daughters of a wealthy family who at that time were living at the now-demolished grand house of Springfield, on Hilperton Road in Trowbridge.

Bessie was born in 1880, at least the fifth child of seven from Bethnal Green-born John Thomas Gramlick and his wife Emily Hornsby. Like most of her siblings (she had five sisters – Emily, Martha, Minnie, Ellen and Mary - and a brother – John Thomas), she was born in Vienna, where her father made a good living as a high-class plumber, putting in water supplies and indoor plumbing for grand palaces across Austria and Poland in the later 19th century. Flushing toilets and indoor running water were gaining popularity across this period, and John Thomas Gramlick was in the right position to make money from the desire for this convenience.

The family were part of a good number of English people – despite their Germanic-sounding surname (it is sometimes spelled Gramlich in Austria), John Thomas appears to have been English for several generations back – in the Austrian capital, and seem to have played a big part in that society. He is known to have been a founder of the Vienna Cricket and Football Club. He also founded the first international football club cup competition – the Challenge Cup – for the sport.

At some point around the turn of the century, Bessie and her family returned to the UK. Her father had retired from running the plumbing business full time, and left his son John Thomas junior in charge. They first went to Clevedon, on the Bristol channel in North Somerset, but the 1901 census has the family holidaying at a boarding house in Brighton. They then became tenants at Springfield – with an option to buy it – in the autumn of 1901.

Springfield was a large residence on the Hilperton Road in Trowbridge, built in about the 1840s. Prior to the Gramlick family living there, it had been the home of Brigadier-General George Llewellen Palmer, who had moved up to the larger manor house at Lackham, near Chippenham. And prior to that it was the home of William Stancomb Esq. and his family. Both Stancomb and Palmer were two of the principal clothiers' dynasties in Trowbridge.

By autumn 1902 they were decorating the parish church for harvest festival, and by May 1904 when Bessie's mother died the family were clearly well settled in Trowbridge society.

The local newspaper report of Emily (Emmy) Gramlick's funeral reports on many tributes from local people, and floral arrangements from all daughters including 'Little Bess' – a pet name for Bessie. She also sometimes seems to have been known as Bessl, in a nod to the family having spent time in a German-speaking country. The funeral was attended by a whole houseful of servants and friends.

There are sporadic reports of the family in newspapers of the first decade of the 20th century. The Misses Gramlick appear to have played tennis, cricket and hockey among other society women, and attended grand weddings – Bessie contributed a fancy cushion as a present to one, while her sisters offered a butter knife. There is also a report of Bessie being a fair amateur actress in a production of Red Riding Hood at Staverton School Room in 1906, which involved various of her sisters. Bessie played the Queen of Sylvania, and reportedly acted it in a 'graceful and artistic way'. At least one of the sisters played the piano well enough to perform solos in public entertainments, and probably all of them had been taught the instrument.

The first official mentions of the early 20th century women's suffrage movement in the Trowbridge area newspapers are a couple of meetings in 1909 held under the auspices of the Bath Women's Suffrage Society. Mr E Pinckney, Chairman of the Finance Committee of Wiltshire County Council, had declared at a meeting at Trowbridge Town Hall in 1909 that he was in support of women's suffrage. There was also an advertised meeting at the town hall council chamber in October 1909, with a couple of speakers brought in from Bath – a Miss Von Donop and a Miss Wheelwright – and Reverend Geoffrey Ramsey, who was a member of the Men's League for Women's Suffrage. Admission was free, and apparently the venue was packed. It is unknown whether Bessie or any of her sisters attended, but it seems likely that they might have done.

A reception for women to discuss votes for women was held by the WSPU at Trowbridge Town Hall on 14 March 1911, but while the invitation came from Lillian Dove-Willcox - who had apparently travelled from Bristol to work in the town as joint organiser for the WSPU - there was no mention of Bessie's connection to the movement at this instance. Lillian Dove-Willcox had been in and out of prison in London during 1909 as part of the WSPU campaign, for protesting and parading, and had been on hunger strike. She also replaced fellow prominent suffragette Annie Kenney as secretary of Bristol WSPU in 1911.

Bessie's name appearing as the co-chair of the West Wilts WSPU in 1911-12 is concurrent with her appearance on the 1911 census, on the night of 2 April 1911. On this document she is 30 and has no profession – like all of her sisters. She's given by her full name Elizabeth. All her sisters are at home, and unmarried. There is no sign that she had attempted to evade the census takers, like other WSPU members.

Lillian Dove-Willcox was a census evader. She travelled from Trowbridge in a van that night, heading for Salisbury Plain, so that she was not in a residence to be recorded. Trowbridge town hall officials wrote a return for her on 7 April, after receiving a letter from an Archer Bellingham Esq, describing her whereabouts.

There is no further connection of the WSPU to Bessie Gramlick in the newspapers at the time, though she was also secretary for the local Lawn Tennis Association, and it is likely the duties were similar – organising meetings, writing letters, and gathering support for causes. She may have been involved in organising travel for any speakers at gatherings too.

In 1912, Lillian Dove Willcox left the WSPU organisation as she did not support the arson campaign founded that year. Bessie's views on the movement's actions at this time are open to speculation, as there is no public record of her involvement past the founding of the Trowbridge branch.

In September 1914, Bessie was compelled to write to the local press in Trowbridge, refuting local speculation on the origin of the Gramlick name as it was particularly Germanic at a time when anti-German feelings were on the rise after the outbreak of the First World War that August. She stated, quite rightly, that the Gramlick name had been British for at least three hundred years.

The next record available shows that, like many women of her class at that time, she also volunteered for the Voluntary Red Cross at Trowbridge in February 1916 as part of the Voluntary Aid Detachment hospitals movement during the First World War. This movement provided temporary medical staff at field hospitals set up in town halls and other prominent buildings throughout the country to nurse and rehabilitate soldiers shipped from the front lines. There were all sorts of roles that these volunteers could take on, including cooking and serving and washing-up, right through to active nursing. Bessie worked six hours per week at the Wilts War Hospital Supply Depot, as a member of the British Red Cross work party, and was retained until 1919. She was awarded a VW badge, a volunteer war workers badge, for this. Her sisters Emily, Martha, Mary and Ellen (known as Nella) also worked there alongside her, and the hospital was under the charge of Mabel Soames, of The Grange, Hilperton.

Many of the Gramlick sisters remained unmarried, and living at Springfield, except for her sister Mary in 1921. However, her father's will, enacted around six months after her wedding took place, refers to Mary as a spinster. Her married status probably hadn't had a chance to be updated by the time he died in early 1922. Bessie, Mary and another spinster sister Emily inherited nearly £6,000 and were still given as living at Springfield in Trowbridge.

In the 1920s either she or her sister Emily (who had the same first initial) was in charge of Lifeboat Day in Trowbridge, raising funds for the cause.

Bessie finally married in 1935, when she was around 55 years old. Her husband was John Conyngham McClintock, an ex-Army captain. The marriage was reported in the newspapers as having taken place in St Mary's at Bryanston Square in London, with no bridesmaids, and was probably a quiet affair. Wiltshire newspapers reported the occasion as

Bessie was well-known in the area across the local lawn tennis games. John was Irish-born, 18 years her senior, and a widower with grown-up children.

The couple lived first in Fleet in Hampshire, and were there for the beginning of the Second World War. John died there in 1942. Bessie subsequently moved to the village of Freshford, on the River Avon near Bath.

Family trees online give Bessie's death, unmarried, as 1951 in Trowbridge. However, there is no record that backs up this account, and probably arises from the mangling that her Gramlick surname has been given in official marriage registers. She actually died in November 1951 at Freshford, leaving probate to two nephews.

Her sister Emily lived on at Springfield until her death in 1966. The house then seems to have been abandoned, and eventually demolished. Modern housing has been built on the land, but the original gates still stand on Hilperton Road.

References

Bath Chronicle and Weekly Gazette, 23 July 1903 Wedding of Miss Mann at Hilperton

Bath Chronicle and Weekly Gazette, 8 July 1909 Trowbridge: Lawn Tennis Tournament

Bath Chronicle and Weekly Gazette, 9 March 1935 Marriages

British Army, British Red Cross Society Volunteers 1914-1918, held by Findmypast.co.uk

Cheltenham Looker-On, 31 August 1901 'Looker On' visitors' list

Clifton Society, 16 November 1905 Marriages

Clifton Society, 7 August 1913, Wilts Lawn Tennis Tournament

Common Cause, 21 October 1909 Bath

Crawford, E (2013) *The Women's Suffrage Movement in Britain and Ireland: A Regional Survey*, Routledge

Devizes and Wiltshire Gazette, 22 June 1905 Girls' Friendly Society

Devizes and Wilts Advertiser, 10 June 1909 Sports and Pastimes: Cricket

England and Wales 1921 census, held by Findmypast.co.uk

England & Wales, Civil Registration Birth Index, 1916-2007, held by Ancestry.co.uk

England & Wales, Civil Registration Marriage Index, 1916-2005, held by Ancestry.co.uk

England & Wales, Civil Registration Death Index, 1916-2007, held by Ancestry.co.uk

First Vienna Football Club, *History of First Vienna Football Club* 1894, at https://

www.firstviennafc.at/vereinsgeschichte.html?lang=en (accessed 28.7.2024)
London Metropolitan Archives, held by Ancestry.co.uk
Simpkin, J (1997) *Lillian Dove Willcox in Spartacus Educational*, at https://spartacus-educational.com/WdoveL.htm (accessed 28.7.2024)
Somerset Guardian and Radstock Observer, 9 May 1952, £4,400 Estate
Trowbridge Chronicle, 26 October 1901 A tenant for Springfield
UK Census collection, held by Ancestry.co.uk
Western Daily Press, 4 March 1935, Capt. J. C. McClintock—Miss E. Gramlick, in London
Wiltshire, England, Church of England Births and Baptisms, 1813-1922, held by Ancestry.co.uk
Wiltshire, England, Church of England Marriages and Banns, 1754-1916, held by Ancestry.co.uk
Wiltshire, England, Church of England Deaths and Burials, 1813-1922 held by Ancestry.co.uk
Wiltshire Telegraph, 6 May 1916 Wiltshire Arts and Crafts: The Wilton Exhibition
Wiltshire Times and Trowbridge Advertiser, 18 October 1902 Harvest festivals
Wiltshire Times and Trowbridge Advertiser, 14 May 1904 Death of Mrs Gramlick
Wiltshire Times and Trowbridge Advertiser, 21 May 1904 Funeral of Mrs Gramlich
Wiltshire Times and Trowbridge Advertiser, 6 January 1906 Staverton: Fairy play & entertainment at the schoolroom
Wiltshire Times and Trowbridge Advertiser, 25 August 1906 Steeple Ashton: Successful garden fete at the vicarage
Wiltshire Times and Trowbridge Advertiser, 15 September 1906 Pretty wedding at the parish church
Wiltshire Times and Trowbridge Advertiser, 22 February 1908 Wingfield concert
Wiltshire Times and Trowbridge Advertiser, 14 November 1908 West Wilts Moonrakers Ladies Hockey Club
Wiltshire Times and Trowbridge Advertiser, 20 June 1908 Trowbridge Lawn Tennis Tournament
Wiltshire Times and Trowbridge Advertiser, 9 October 1909 Women's suffrage meeting
Wiltshire Times and Trowbridge Advertiser, 16 October 1909 The women's suffrage movement: interesting meeting at the town hall
Wiltshire Times and Trowbridge Advertiser, 12 September 1914 Unfounded statements
Wiltshire Times and Trowbridge Advertiser, 2 October 1920 Trowbridge: Death of Mr Tubb Thomas
Wiltshire Times and Trowbridge Advertiser, 7 December 1929, Lifeboat Day

Martha Bennett

With the advent of the NHS, and better maternal and social care, in addition to many labour-saving devices for housework, the role of a monthly nurse has become quite lost in obscurity.

However, back in the days where women were supposed to have both a confinement before birth and a lying-in period of rest – of at least nine days if not longer – after giving birth, a monthly nurse was an extremely desirable person to employ. She was paid to assist a woman and her family in the pre-and-post-partum period at home, as most children were born in houses rather than hospitals or maternity facilities.

Today, her role might be confused with that of a midwife, and it is certain that she was usually involved in the actual birth, alongside others including those who did give their professions as midwives. However, she was usually employed by the family both a little before and for quite a while after the birth occurred too, and a more modern term for the role might be a post-partum doula-cum-servant.

Invariably an older woman, a monthly nurse would also assist with some of the body effluent after a birth, do some care for the baby, and look after the new mother, making sure that she was well-nourished and rested as she was healing, and not having to get up to tend to household duties that could be attended to by others.

Household jobs still needed to be done, and men would generally not do them (either by design, as being seen to undertake 'women's work' was emasculating, or by sheer ignorance), so they'd either get a female relative to help out, or pay a monthly nurse for a period of time if they could afford it.

Sometimes the monthly nurse would also assist with laying out the dead, as a high infant mortality rate meant that stillbirths or deaths in the first few days and weeks were a frequent occurrence. Or the new mother might succumb to puerperal fever – a bacterial infection of the reproductive tract that could develop into something life-threatening in the days before antibiotics.

Often, the monthly nurse would live with the family for the duration of her employment, a period which had led to the job title, as they generally stayed for about a month.

Invariably, the monthly nurse was someone who had had all her children and raised them to a reasonable degree of independence – so therefore could leave their own family and jobs to a young adult daughter while she went out and earned money for the family. Sometimes she was married, with a husband at home, and sometimes she was widowed. Usually, she came from the working class, but was without any moral stain on her character. On occasion, she was a younger woman working before her marriage, though this was considerably rarer. And sometimes she was an older unmarried woman who had decided that maternity nursing was her calling. Martha Bennett, of Southwick, to the south-west of Trowbridge, fell into this latter category.

The other characteristic that invariably unites the women who became monthly nurses is their distinct lack of medical training before taking up the profession, and Martha was no different in this. She had been a cloth weaver before she became a monthly nurse. There was no examination or certificate that women had to acquire before beginning work, though there were attempts to regulate and train as the 20th century drew on.

They merely relied on community recommendation and their own reputation, and those who were mothers themselves could draw upon some of their experiences. Many would have been involved at several births for relatives and friends, as extra people would be called in. More often than not, basic medical care and invalid nursing would have fallen to women as part of household duties, as doctors were expensive, so a monthly nurse would have had plenty of experience on the job. And preparing of meals and doing household tasks were ubiquitous in everyone's home, so performing them in another family house and being paid for that role would have been a great draw.

Isabella Beeton's book on household management, from 1861, advises that the family's choice of monthly nurse should be a woman of good and upstanding moral character. She goes on to say that she should be honest, sober and noiseless in her movements. This reference to upstanding moral character may have been what attracted Martha to the profession in the first place, as she was deeply religious and supposed not to have ever read any other book than the Bible.

Martha was actually a twin. She and her sister Mary were born in North Bradley in the spring of 1851, to parents John and Eliza Bennett.

They were probably the couple's third pregnancy, and from later accounts it appears that the fact that they were twins was something of a surprise. The family initially seems to have been part of the Church of England, but only their eldest sister Catherine had a baptism in North Bradley church. By the time their brother William came along in 1848, and Martha and Mary, and then their younger siblings Eliza and Job, the family had moved to religious non-conformism of some flavour, probably Baptist like many in that parish at the time.

Martha's father John was an agricultural labourer. Her mother, Eliza, worked as a hand loom weaver at one of the cloth mills in Trowbridge alongside bringing up her growing family. She probably had immobile babies with her while she worked, breastfeeding them on demand while at the loom, and relied upon wider family members to care for toddlers when that became impractical.

Martha worked at the cloth mills too, from at least the age of 10. She appears on the 1861 census as a wool winder, alongside other sister Catherine who had also taken up hand loom weaving. The Education Act which made school attendance compulsory between the ages of 5 and 10 was nineteen years away, so it is very likely that her schooling was minimal and voluntary. This perhaps explains why the only book that she ever read was the Bible, though the newspaper report this claim comes from paints this as a glowing fact of great piety rather than a lack of basic education enabling her to read more widely. Given that her mother was working, it indicates that money was needed for the family, so being employed as a child for a minimal wage is unsurprising.

By the time they were 19, both Martha and her twin Mary were working as domestic servants, which probably brought in a slightly better wage than the cloth mill – though both their mother and younger sister Eliza continued to weave. Their older sister Catherine, known as Kate, had married locally. Around the age of 20, the sisters left whichever church they had been attending, and became members of the Providence Baptist Chapel at Southwick, being baptised in the village stream. However, the foray into domestic service did not last, and both twins returned to the cloth mills before 1881 and were still there on the 1891 census. Mary, at least, worked at the mill owned by Brown and Palmer, and would pull a twelve-hour shift, from 6am until 6pm. She would walk the miles between their Southwick home and the mill before and after work. It is likely that Martha did something very similar while working at the mills.

At some point after 1891, Martha made the change to monthly nursing. She does not appear to have done any formal training to make this change, and certainly does not feature on any registered nursing lists. Instead, she may have felt it was a calling from her faith, or a change in her health which meant a move away from the mill atmosphere would be beneficial. She may have been known to local health providers, who could do a certain amount of regulation, but there was nothing in place to ensure quality of care if Martha wanted to become a monthly nurse. She just went and did it.

She doubtless worked for a month or so at a time at many different homes in the area, assisting families as they welcomed new lives. Census records can only show us two such households. In 1901 she was working for carpenter Sirius Stafford at Pole's Hole in Southwick, whose wife Sarah had an unnamed baby daughter aged under a month. In 1911 she was with the family of George Doel, a carriage cleaner for the Great Western Railway, whose wife Mary Ann had a little boy aged under a month. He didn't have a name at that time either.

Twin sister Mary had also registered Martha's presence at home in Southwick on the 1911 census, which the enumerators had not spotted. They had a five-year-old child living with them, Nelson Richmond, who they appeared to be bringing up together. He was quite probably born to a mother who wasn't married, who had given him up for some sort of adoption or fostering arrangement which Martha may have been party to through her work. He later went to live with a family in Worcester.

Mary's erroneous entry for Martha on the 1911 census lists her as a midwife as well as a monthly nurse. This, combined with the presence of Nelson, perhaps shows that she had received some more formally recognised training since she had begun monthly nursing, and – if not certificated – was regarded in the eyes of the medical profession as something more than just an older woman who had decided to chance her arm. She may have spent some time at a lying in hospital or working alongside a midwife or nurse.

The two households that Martha can be observed working in are very much typical for a monthly nurse. Though their care had to be paid for, they were not the preserve of the rich or the newly affluent Victorian middle class. Instead, monthly nurses are invariably found in the homes of farmers and vicars, who would have been the top end of their scale, and then also with tradesmen and publicans, railway workers and shop keepers.

Bessie Bast, a monthly nurse from Salisbury, was working for a pub landlady in 1911 and a railway boiler fireman's family in 1921. Flora Churchill, also in Salisbury in 1911, was with a farmer's wife. Hannah Rose, a monthly nurse in Westbury in 1901, was working for a fish and game dealer's family. Gertrude Sheffard, who was working in Warminster in 1911, helped blacksmith's wife Laura Dewey with her new baby. Ann Fielding, of Warminster, was working for a butcher salesman's family in 1911. Catherine Charlotte Green, originally from Kent, was helping a first-time mother in on a farm at Imber with her new son in 1911. Ellen Lodder, a widowed monthly nurse, was assisting Amy Foyle – the wife of a corn merchant's manager – with her new daughter at Wilton in 1911.

This wider picture of where these women are working shows that monthly nurse services were not typically financially available for those like Martha and Mary's parents, who had been working on the land and the factory, but could be afforded by those only a couple of rungs further up the social ladder. And some of those could have care for the first few children, but as the family grew and money had to be stretched, they would have to manage without.

Those beneath that social bracket would instead rely on the kindness of relatives and neighbours – invariably a mother or mother-in-law would do what she could for the post-partum mother but would also have her own household to manage. And in many cases, a healing woman would get up and take on heavy house duties before she should, putting her on-going health at risk. Many women who had gone through multiple pregnancies with little or poor rest after birth reported problems with veins in their legs, and issues with their uterus and bladder.

In the first couple of decades of the 20th century, social reformers were beginning to focus on the high infant mortality rate, particularly among the working classes, and there were moves to improve and educate around better maternal health. Society sought to move away from what were viewed as the shortcomings of the Victorian age, and educating mothers into better health was part of that. In Salisbury, the Hulse Clinic was founded in 1915 to offer new thinking in maternity services, taking care of mothers and new babies, which is explored more in the chapter on Helen and Grace Bagnall. In London, the Duchess of Marlborough Maternity Hospital was beginning to offer antenatal and infant welfare services around the same time, focusing on boroughs where poverty was at its highest. Marie Stopes, at the time an important academic though now widely discredited as a eugenicist, published *Married Love*, the first book to openly discuss birth control and methods, in 1918. Those attending at a birth were starting to be required to have more formal medical training, rather than being drawn from the community, and the role of monthly nurse began to be amalgamated with that of midwife, eventually disappearing altogether.

It's likely that Martha did not continue working into this new more-medicalised system. By 1921, she had taken retirement, as had her sister Mary, and at the age of 70 called themselves old age pensioners. They lived together in their cottage on the Frome Road in Southwick. They seem to have been fairly spry in retirement though, as they remained active at home and church. Their younger brother Job, who had been a policeman in Brighton, returned to the area on his retirement, and settled in North Bradley.

It was their combined age that brought the pair of them to public attention eventually. On their 87th birthday in May 1938 they were declared the Oldest Twins in England by the local newspaper, the *Wiltshire Times*, who ran a feature on them. Interviewed by their cottage fire, they say that:

> Martha, appropriate for one of her name – took up nursing, and many of the residents of the village now in middle age, were assisted into the world by her ministrations. Her services for maternity and other cases were in great demand… Miss Mary is now the most active of the two and

is a cheerful little lady although her sight is failing. Miss Martha is very deaf. Neither of them go far now, but sometimes when the weather is fine they walk down to the Frome Road, where they see the noisy modern traffic pass by.

Their brother Job, the last of their siblings, died in North Bradley that September, aged 80. Martha and Mary's 88th birthday was also remarked upon in the newspaper in May of 1939.

One of them, and it is impossible to say who without acquiring their death certificates, died on the 15th of November 1939. The Wiltshire Times said it was Martha, but the *Daily Herald* and the *Somerset Standard* reported Mary's death. The twin that was left was in good health in one report, and in very poor health in another. Whoever remained died in the following weeks before the end of 1939, as both death certificates fall into the same quarter of registration. The *Daily Herald* reported that neither twin had ever been fitted for their Second World War gas mask.

References

Adams, C. (1982), *Ordinary Lives*, Virago
Beeton, I. (1861), *The Book of Household Management ... Also, Sanitary, Medical, & Legal Memoranda; With a History of the Origin, Properties, and Uses of All Things Connected With Home Life and Comfort*. London, S. O.
Daily Herald, 17 November 1939, Martha and Mary
Davies, M.L. (1915), *Maternity: Letters from Working Women*, Hogarth Press
England & Wales, 1921 census, held by Findmypast.co.uk
England & Wales, Civil Registration Birth Index, 1837-1915, held by Ancestry.co.uk
England & Wales, Civil Registration Death Index, 1916-2007, held by Ancestry.co.uk
Gregory, P (2023) *Normal Women*, Collins
Reeves, M.P. (1913), *Round About A Pound A Week*, London: G Bell and Sons
Somerset Standard, 24 November 1939, Lived together for 88 years
Stopes, M.C. (1918), *Married Love*, Fifield & Co
UK Census Collection, held by Ancestry.co.uk
Wiltshire, England, Church of England Births and Baptisms, 1813-1922, held by Ancestry.co.uk
Wiltshire, England, Church of England Marriages and Banns, 1754-1916, held by Ancestry.co.uk
Wiltshire Times and Trowbridge Advertiser, 21 May 1938, Martha and Mary

Wiltshire Times and Trowbridge Advertiser, 3 September 1938, Death of Mr J Bennett
Wiltshire Times and Trowbridge Advertiser, 27 May 1939, Southwick: The Oldest Twins
Wiltshire Times and Trowbridge Advertiser, 18 November 1939, Deaths
Wiltshire Times, 18 November 1939, Southwick: 'One Shall Be Taken'

Index

Adcock, Miss 13
Alderbury 57, 58, 60, 61
Alresford, Old 69
Amesbury 1, 43, 96, 101
Australia 29, 30, 33
Austria 126
Awdry family 23
Aylward, Amy 75-81
Ayrshire 21, 22, 26

Bagnall, Helen and Grace 28-38
Bannerdown House, Batheaston 25
Barford St Martin 57, 120
Bath 6, 12, 17, 25, 26, 31, 36, 69–71, 83, 91, 92, 104, 107, 128, 130
Bath Women's Suffrage Society 128
Batheaston 25
Beaton, Isabella 133
Bedfordshire 28
Bellefield, Trowbridge 70-73
Bemerton Lodge 120
Bennett, Martha 132-9
Berkshire 28, 42
Bermuda 50
Bethnal Green 126
Bishop's Lavington 107
Bournemouth 44
Bowerhill 82
Bown, Emma 56-65
Bradford-on-Avon 3, 5, 14, 54, 82-5, 87-8
Bradley's Buildings, Bath 91
Bremen 50
Brewery Tap, Trowbridge 104
Bridgman, Alice 12
Brighton 33, 127, 137

Bristol 31, 78, 126–28
Broadmoor asylum 87, 115
Brompton Hospital, London 97
Buckinghamshire 36
Butler Education Act, 1944 17, 43

Caen Hill, Devizes 7
Cambridge 79
Canada 10, 16, 101
Cape Town 32, 121
Cardiff 7, 48–52, 54, 76
Casement, Mary Edith 13
Castle Steam Laundry, Warminster 47, 52-55
Charlwood, Surrey 42
Cheapside, London 106
Chelmsford 15
Chichester Cathedral 76
Chippenham 23, 47, 90, 127
Chorlton, Manchester 10
Clapcott, Berks. 42
Clark, Dorcas 66-74
Clark, J & T, Mill Owners, Trowbridge 67-68
Clevedon 127
Clydach Vale 99
Clyffe Hall, Littleton Pannell 42
Codford 61
Cornwall 22
Corsley 2
Coryton, Devon 118
Cowbridge, Glamorgan 113
Crufts dog show 23

Darlington 50
Dartmoor 118

Dauntsey House, West Lavington 43
Davies, Maud Frances 2
Dawlish 118–20
Devizes 7, 22, 36, 42, 43, 47, 59, 64, 82, 83, 87, 110, 112–14, 121
Devizes Prison 64, 112, 113
Devon 12, 13, 92, 118, 120
Didsbury, Manchester 10
Dick, Kerr Ladies Football Club 40
Diocesan High School for Girls, Auckland 29-30, 32
Divorce 86, 103-107
Dorset 13, 41, 43, 44, 85
Douglas, Mary Alice 31, 33
Dove-Willcox, Lillian 128
Downton 57
Dowson, Mrs Aubrey (Phillis) 2
Dunkerton 91, 107
Duchess of Marlborough Maternity Hospital, London 137

Edinburgh 21
Electoral Act 1893, New Zealand 30
Essex 15, 79
Eton 76
Exeter 118

FA ban on women's football 39
Favilli, Elena & Cavallo, Francesca 3
Fawcett, Henry (MP) 33
Fawcett, Millicent 33
Fisherton Anger gaol 111, 114
Fisherton House Asylum, Salisbury 87-88, 121
Folkestone 13
Fovant 103
Foxhanger Bridge, Rowde 7
Freemantle, Ann 56-65
Freshford, Somerset 36, 130
Frome 54, 66
Fugglestone St Peter 61, 121
Fuller, Emily (née Hicks-Beach) 13

Gambia 10
Gibraltar 51
Gladstone Solomon, Gwladys 33-34

Godolphin School, Salisbury 28-29, 31-35
Goodfellow, Emma and Ann 56-65
Goodfellow, Jane 103-8
Gramlick, Bessy 126-31
Gravesend 79
Great Cumberwell 72
Grosmont Iron Works, Whitby 28
Guildford 105

Hackney 33
Hallé, Charles 76
Hamilton, Christian 21-7
Hammersmith 52
Hampshire 41, 44, 69, 130
Hampstead 80
Harefield, Midddlesex 42
Hassan, Elsie 47-55
Hay, Lizzie Hilda 9-20
Heaton Norris, Lancs. 11
Heytesbury 103
Hicks-Beach, Lady Lucy 13
Hilperton 129
Hulse Clinic, Salisbury 32-33
Hurdcott (Winterbourne Earls) 100–102
Hurdcott House 120

Ilfracombe 92
Imber 136
Ireland 22
Islington 21

J & T Clark, Mill Owners, Trowbridge 67-68
Judd, Harriet 109-17

Kennel Club 23
Kennet and Avon Canal 7, 64
Kenney, Annie 128
Kensington 2, 64, 122–3
Kent 13, 136
Kilburn 98

La Rochelle, France 22
Lackham 127

Lake, Wilsford 101
Lancashire 11
Lavington, Market 36, 106
Lavington, West 3, 40–45, 107
Leech, John Henry 120
Lethbridge, Sybil Campbell 2
Liberia 10
Limpley Stoke 59
Lincolnshire 70
Little Bytham, Lincs. 70
Little Langford 44
Littleton Pannell 41, 42, 44
Littleton Wood, Semington 82-83
Liverpool 10, 13, 50
Llandaff Cathedral 76
Lodge, Dorothy May 96-102
Ludgershall 47
Lullington 66

McClintock, Bessy 126-31
Maidenhead 72
Manchester 10–12
Manningford Abbots 109, 113, 114
Marystow, Devon 118
Matrimonial Causes Act, 1857 105
Men's League for Women's Suffrage 128
Metzler and Co. Pianos 75
Mexico 123
Millbank Prison 114-115
Milton Mount College, Essex 79
Moray Lodge, Campden Hill, Kensington 122
Mossley, Lancs. 11
Mother's Union 69

National Union of Women's Suffrage Societies 33
National Union of Women Workers 32
Neston Park, Corsham 13
Netheravon 13
New York 24, 122, 123
New Zealand 29, 30, 32, 36, 41
Newman, Thirza 109-17
Newport, Mon. 43
Nightingale, Florence 96

Noad, Freelove Priscilla 82-9
Norman-Neruda, Wilma 76
Norris, Phyllis Irene 2
North Bradley 134, 137, 138
North Middlesex hospital 100
Northamptonshire 28
Nottinghamshire 69
Notton, Lacock 23

Offences Against the Person Act, 1828 57
Offences Against the Person Act, 1861 56, 60, 62
Ottley, Alice 28
Oxford 28

Paddington Hospital 97
Painswick, Glos. 36
Palestine 32
Pankhurst, Kate 3
Paris 70
Parr, Lily 40
Pattingham, Staffs. 28
Pearce/Pierce, Dorcas 66-74
Pengelly, Ellen 118-25
Penzance 22
Pewsey 112, 113
Pleurisy 6
Plough Inn, Bradford-on-Avon 83-85
Plymouth 78
Poland 47, 126
Pomeranians 21, 23, 24, 25
Poole 43
Portsea Island 107
Portsmouth 106, 107
Possart, Elsie 47-55
Public Health (Tuberculosis) Act, 1921 101

Queen's Nursing Institute 96, 100

Ramsey, Isle of Man 10
Randegger, Alberto 77
Redlynch 58, 59
Rhondda UDC 99
Richmond upon Thames 42

Roentgen Ray apparatus 93
Roundway Lunatic Asylum, Devizes 87, 121
Rowde 82
Royal Academy of Music, London 77
Royal Chiswick Laundry, Chiswick 52
Rozelle House, Ayrshire 22
Russell, Alys 35
Ryde 78, 81

St Pancras 99, 100, 122
Salisbury 1–3, 13, 28, 31–33, 35, 42–44, 47, 57, 61, 75–79, 87–88, 94, 96, 101, 103, 109–11, 113, 117, 120, 128, 136, 137
Salisbury and South Wilts Women's Suffrage Society 33
Sarum Choral Society 75
Schlochau (Człuchów), Prussia 47
Scotland 21, 22, 73
Seend Manor 22, 23, 24
Semington 82
Sex Disqualification (Removal) Act, 1919 45, 98-99
Sheffield 78
Shore, Jane 103-8
Sims, Freelove Priscilla 82-9
Smith, Mary 13
Smith, Susanna 90-5
Somerset 57, 91, 107, 127
South Wales Steam Laundry, Cardiff 51-52
South Wraxall 72
Southampton 121
Southwick 133, 135, 137
Springfield, Trowbridge 126-127
Staffordshire 28, 60
Stanwick, Notts. 69, 70
Staverton 127
Stockton 103
Stockwell, London 122, 123
Sturminster, Dorset 41
Stuttgart Conservatoire 77
Sumner, Mary 69
Surrey 42, 114
Sussex 14

Sutton, Harriet 109-17
Swansea 48
Swindon 47, 115

Tadd, Susannah, 5-8
Thisbe, Cardiff East Dock 49
Tiger Bay, Cardiff 48
Tilshead 44
Tisbury 61, 62, 88
Tottenham 98
Training School of Domestic Science, Bath 12
Trowbridge 3, 10, 12, 13, 16–17, 45, 54, 66–72, 83, 84, 103, 104, 107, 126–30, 133, 134

Utterson, Elizabeth 90
Uxbridge 42

Vagrancy Act 1824 109
Vauxhall 106, 107

Wales 43, 47–48, 50, 51, 56, 113
Wardour 88
Warminster 3, 47, 52, 54, 90–94, 103, 136
Warminster Cottage Hospital 92-94
Wastfield, Freelove Priscilla 82-9
West Lavington Ladies Football Team 39-46
West Lavington Sports Club 41
Westbury 54, 136
Westwood, Bradford-on-Avon 5
Weymouth 85
Whitby 28
Wight, Isle of 78
Willson, Katherine Agnes 14, 15
Wilton 136
Wiltshire School of Cookery and Domestic Economy, Trowbridge 9, 12-17
Wimborne Minster 44
Winchester 62
Winterbourne Earls 96, 100, 101
Winterslow 43
Withington, Manchester 10

Woodford 100, 101
Woking Female Prison 114
Women's Social & Political Union 126
Woolwich Union Infirmary, London 96
Worcester 28–31, 135
Worcester High School for Girls, (Alice Ottley School) 28
Worton 43

Wurttemberg, Germany 77
Wycombe Abbey Public School for Girls 36
Wyke Regis, Dorset 85
Wylye river and valley 44, 54, 103

Yipsing, Ellen 118-25
Yorkshire 28, 72

About the author ~~

LUCY WHITFIELD is a hands-on creative history practitioner and research obsessive.

People and their stories are at the heart of everything that she does, whether that be introducing adults to their ordinary extraordinary female ancestors, educating school children about skills their forebears would have possessed, demonstrating medieval headdresses and hand spinning at a family open day, or teaching workshops on the sailor's hornpipe at a folk festival.

She is the founder of *The Women Who Made Me* project, which researches and profiles ordinary extraordinary women across history and aims to inspire people to re-evaluate and reconnect with their female relatives, and her discoveries have been broadcast on BBC radio and exhibited in museums. She regularly talks to groups about her work, and displays at museums and history centres.

Lucy always says that she collects interesting women, both personally and professionally, and is usually knee deep in researching her latest discovery. She also has an archaeology degree, used to be a journalist, and once made a crop circle.

But that's another story…

www.lucywhitfieldhistorian.co.uk

www.ingramcontent.com/pod-product-compliance
Lightning Source LLC
Chambersburg PA
CBHW062111080426
42734CB00012B/2824